Dr Kennerley is the author of *Overcoming Anxiety*, the *Overcoming Anxiety Self-Help Course* and *Overcoming Childhood Trauma*. She qualified in Clinical Psychology at Oxford, where she also trained to become a cognitive therapist. She is one of the founder members of the Oxford Cognitive Therapy Centre (OCTC). Currently, she works as a consultant within OCTC, where she is the lead clinician of a specialist clinic in cognitive therapy. Helen has presented many workshops in her area of expertise both nationally and internationally. In 2002 she was shortlisted by the British Association for Behaviour and Cognitive Psychotherapies for the award for most influential female cognitive therapist in Britain.

The aim of the **Overcoming** series is to enable people with a range of
common problems and disorders to take control of their own recovery program.
Each title, with its specially tailored program, is devised by a practicing
clinician using the latest techniques of cognitive behavioral therapy –
techniques which have been shown to be highly effective in changing the
way patients think about themselves and their problems.
The series was initiated in 1993 by Peter Cooper, Professor of Psychology
at Reading University and Research Fellow at the University of Cambridge
in the UK whose original volume on overcoming bulimia nervosa and
binge-eating continues to help many people in the USA, the UK and Europe.

Titles in the series include:

OVERCOMING ANGER AND IRRITABILITY
OVERCOMING ANOREXIA NERVOSA
OVERCOMING BODY IMAGE PROBLEMS
OVERCOMING BULIMIA NERVOSA AND BINGE-EATING
OVERCOMING CHILDHOOD TRAUMA
OVERCOMING CHRONIC FATIGUE
OVERCOMING CHRONIC PAIN
OVERCOMING COMPULSIVE GAMBLING
OVERCOMING DEPERSONALIZATION AND FEELINGS OF UNREALITY
OVERCOMING DEPRESSION
OVERCOMING GRIEF
OVERCOMING INSOMNIA AND SLEEP PROBLEMS
OVERCOMING LOW SELF-ESTEEM
OVERCOMING MOOD SWINGS
OVERCOMING OBSESSIVE COMPULSIVE DISORDER
OVERCOMING PANIC
OVERCOMING PARANOID AND SUSPICIOUS THOUGHTS
OVERCOMING RELATIONSHIP PROBLEMS
OVERCOMING SEXUAL PROBLEMS
OVERCOMING SOCIAL ANXIETY AND SHYNESS
OVERCOMING TRAUMATIC STRESS
OVERCOMING WEIGHT PROBLEMS
OVERCOMING WORRY
OVERCOMING YOUR CHILD'S FEARS AND WORRIES
OVERCOMING YOUR CHILD'S SHYNESS AND SOCIAL ANXIETY
OVERCOMING YOUR SMOKING HABIT

All titles in the series are available by mail order.
Please see the order form at the back of this book.
www.overcoming.co.uk

OVERCOMING ANXIETY

*A self-help guide using
Cognitive Behavioral Techniques*

HELEN KENNERLEY

Robinson
LONDON

Constable & Robinson Ltd
3 The Lanchesters
162 Fulham Palace Road
London W6 9ER
www.constablerobinson.com

First published by Robinson Publishing Ltd, 1997

This edition published by Robinson, an imprint of
Constable & Robinson Ltd, 2009

A copy of the British Library Cataloguing in
Publication Data is available from the British Library.

Important Note

This book is not intended as a substitute for medical advice or treatment.
Any person with a condition requiring medical attention should consult
a qualified medical practitioner or suitable therapist.

ISBN 978-1-8490-107-1-9

Printed and bound in EU.

3 5 7 9 10 8 6 4

Table of contents

Foreword

Many, perhaps the majority, of those who go to see their family doctor have some type of psychological problem which makes them anxious or unhappy. There may be a fairly obvious reason for this – the loneliness of widowhood or the stresses of bringing up a family – or it may be that their mental state is part of their personality, something they were born with or a reaction to traumatic experiences in their lives. Despite being so common, I soon discovered after starting in general practice over ten years ago that this type of mental disturbance (usually described as a *neurosis* to distinguish it from the *psychosis* of those with a serious mental illness like schizophrenia) is particularly difficult to deal with. What are the options? Well, there are always drugs – minor tranquillizers, antidepressants and sleeping pills. It is certainly easy enough to write a prescription and more often than not the patient feels a lot better as a result, but there is no getting away from the fact that drugs are a chemical fix. Sometimes this is all that is necessary to tide someone over a difficult period, but more usually the same old problems recur when the drugs are discontinued.

The alternatives to drugs are the 'talking therapies', ranging from psychoanalysis to counselling, that seek to sort out the underlying cause of anxiety or unhappiness. Psychoanalysis is out of the question for many, being too prolonged – often lasting for years – and too expensive. Counselling certainly can be helpful for no other reason than that unburdening one's soul to a sympathetic listener is invariably therapeutic. But once the counselling sessions were over, I got the impression it was only a matter of time before the psychological distress reappeared.

Here, then, is one of the great paradoxes of modern medicine. Doctors can now transplant hearts, replace arthritic hips and cure meningitis but, confronted by the commonest reason why people seek their advice, they have remarkably little to offer. And then a couple of years ago I started to hear about a new type of psychological treatment – cognitive therapy – which, it was claimed, was not only straightforward but demonstrably effective. I was initially sceptical as I found it difficult to imagine what sort of breakthrough insight into human psychology should lie behind such remarkable claims. The human brain is, after all, the most complex entity in existence, so it would seem unlikely that someone had suddenly, at the end of the twentieth century, found the key that unlocked the mysteries of neuroses – a key that had eluded human understanding for hundreds of years.

The central insight of cognitive therapy is not, it emerges, a new discovery, but rather is based on the profound observation originally formulated by the French philosopher Descartes that the essential feature of human consciousness was 'cogito ergo sum' – 'I think therefore I am.' We are our thoughts and the contents of our thoughts have a major influence on our emotions. Cognitive therapy is based on the principle that certain types of thought that we have about ourselves – whether, at its simplest, we are loved or wanted or despised or boring – have a major effect on the way we perceive the world. If we feel unloved, the world will appear unloving, and then every moment of every day our sense of being unloved is confirmed. That, after all, is what depression is all about. These types of thoughts are called 'automatic thoughts' because they operate on the margins of our consciousness as a continual sort of internal monologue. If these thoughts are identified and brought out into the open then the state of mind that they sustain, whether anxiety or depression or any of the other neuroses, can begin to be resolved.

So this type of therapy is called 'cognitive' because it is primarily about changing our thoughts about ourselves, the world and the future. The proof of the pudding, as they say, is in the eating and the very fact that this type of therapy has been shown to work so well, in countless well-controlled studies, is powerful confirmation that the underlying insight that our thoughts lie behind, and sustain, neurotic illnesses is in essence correct.

Nonetheless, some may be forgiven for having misgivings. The concept of cognitive therapy takes some getting used to and it is certainly hard to credit that complex psychological problems can be explained by such an apparently simple concept. There is perhaps an understandable impression that it all sounds a bit oversimplified or trite, that it fails to get to the root cause of the source of anxiety or depression.

So it is necessary to dig a bit deeper to examine the origins of cognitive therapy, and perhaps the easiest way of doing this is to compare it with what for many is the archetype of all forms of psychotherapy – psychoanalysis. Psycho-analysis claims to identify the source of neuroses in the long-forgotten and repressed traumas of early childhood, so it is less concerned with thoughts themselves than with the hidden meaning which (it claims) underlies them. The important question, though, is whether psychoanalysis does make people better, or at least less unhappy. Many people certainly believe they have been helped, but when Professor Gavin Andrews of the University of New South Wales reviewed all the studies in which the outcome of psycho-analysis had been objectively measured in the *British Journal of Psychiatry* in 1994, he was unable to show that it worked any better than 'just talking'.

In cognitive therapy, the importance of human thoughts lies precisely in their content and how that influences the way a person feels about themselves, a point well illus-trated by one of its early pioneers, Aaron Beck. Back in the 1960s, while practising as a psychoanalyst in Philadelphia, Beck was treating a young woman with an anxiety state which he initially interpreted in true psychoanalytic fashion as being due to a failure to resolve sexual conflict arising from problems in childhood. During one session he noticed that his patient seemed particularly uneasy and, on enquiring why, it emerged she felt embarrassed because she thought she was expressing herself badly and that she sounded trite and foolish. 'These self-evaluative thoughts were very striking,' Beck recalled, 'because she was actually very articulate.' Probing further he found that this false pattern of thinking – that she was dull and uninteresting – permeated all her relationships. He concluded that her chronic anxiety had little to do with her sex life but rather arose from a constant state of dread that her lover might desert her because he found her as uninteresting as she thought herself to be.

Over the next few years, Beck found that he was able to identify similar and quite predictable patterns of thinking in nearly all his patients. For the first time he realized that he was getting inside his patients' minds and beginning to see the world as they experienced it, something he had been unable to do in all his years as a psychoanalyst. From that perspective he went on to develop the principles of cognitive therapy.

Compared to psychoanalysis, cognitive therapy certainly does appear much simpler, but we should not take this to mean that it is less profound. The central failure of the founders of psychoanalysis was that they did not recognize the true significance of thoughts in human neurosis. Once that significance was grasped by those like Aaron Beck, then human psychological disorders became more readily understandable and therefore simpler, but it is the simplicity of an elegant scientific hypothesis that more fully explains the facts. It can't be emphasized too strongly the enormous difference that cognitive therapy has made. Now it is possible to explain quite straightforwardly what is wrong in such a way that people are reassured, while allowing them to be optimistic that their problems can be resolved. Here, at last, is a talking therapy that works.

Professor Gavin Andrews in his review in the *British Journal of Psychiatry* identified cognitive therapy as 'the treatment of choice' in generalized anxiety, obsessive compulsive disorders and depression. It has in addition been shown to be effective in the treatment of eating disorders, panic attacks and even in the management of marital and sexual difficulties, in chronic pain syndromes and many emotional disorders of childhood. Its contribution to the alleviation of human suffering is remarkable.

James Le Fanu, GP

Introduction

Why cognitive behavior therapy?

Over the past two or three decades, there has been something of a revolution in the field of psychological treatment. Freud and his followers had a major impact on the way in which psychological therapy was conceptualized, and psychoanalysis and psychodynamic psychotherapy domiated the field for the first half of this century. So, long-term treatments were offered which were designed to uncover the childhood roots of personal problems – offered, that is, to those who could afford it. There was some attempt by a few health service practitioners with a public conscience to modify this form of treatment (by, for example, offering short-term treatment or group therapy), but the demand for help was so great that this had little impact. Also, whilst numerous case histories can be found of people who are convinced that psychotherapy did help them, practitioners of this form of therapy showed remarkably little interest in demonstrating that what they were offering their patients was, in fact, helpful.

As a reaction to the exclusivity of psychodynamic therapies and the slender evidence for its usefulness, in the 1950s and 1960s a set of techniques was developed, broadly collectively termed 'behavior therapy'. These techniques shared two basic features. First, they aimed to remove symptoms (such as anxiety) by dealing with those symptoms themselves, rather than their deep-seated underlying historical causes. Second, they were techniques, loosely related to what laboratory psychologists were finding out about the mechanisms of learning, which were formulated in testable terms. Indeed, practitioners of behavior therapy were committed to using techniques of proven value or, at worst, of a form which could potentially be put to test. The area where these techniques proved of most value was in the treatment of anxiety disorders, especially specific phobias (such as fear of animals or heights) and agoraphobia, both notoriously difficult to treat using conventional psychotherapies.

After an initial flush of enthusiasm, discontent with behavior therapy grew. There were a number of reasons for this, an important one of which was the fact that behavior therapy did not deal with the internal thoughts which were so obviously central to the distress that patients were experiencing. In this context, the fact that behavior therapy proved so inadequate when it came to the treatment of depression highlighted the need for major revision. In the late 1960s and early 1970s a treatment was developed specificially for depression called 'cognitive therapy'. The pioneer in this enterprise was an American psychiatrist, Professor Aaron T. Beck, who developed a theory of depression which emphasized the importance of people's depressed styles of thinking. He also specified a new form of therapy. It would not be an exaggeration to say that Beck's work has changed the nature of psychotherapy, not just for depression but for a range of psychological problems.

In recent years the cognitive techniques introduced by Beck have been merged with the techniques developed earlier by the behavior therapists to produce a body of theory and practice which has come to be known as 'cognitive behavior therapy'. There are two main reasons why this form of treatment has come to be so important within the field of psychotherapy. First, cognitive therapy for depression, as originally described by Beck and developed by his successors, has been subjected to the strictest scientific testing; and it has been found to be a highly successful treatment for a significant proportion of cases of depression. Not only has it proved to be as effective as the best alternative treatments (except in the most severe cases, where medication is required), but some studies suggest that people treated successfully with cognitive behavior therapy are less likely to experience a later recurrence of their depression than people treated successfully with other forms of therapy (such as antidepressant medication). Second, it has become clear that specific patterns of thinking are associated with a range of psychological problems and that treatments which deal with these styles of thinking are highly effective. So, specific cognitive behavioral treatments have been developed for anxiety disorders, like panic disorder, generalized anxiety disorder, specific phobias and social phobia, obsessive compulsive disorders, and hypochondriasis (health anxiety), as well as for other conditions such as compulsive gambling, alcohol and drug addiction, and eating disorders like bulimia nervosa and binge-eating disorder. Indeed, cognitive behavioral techniques have a wide application beyond the narrow categories of psychological disorders: they have been applied effectively, for example, to helping people with low self-esteem and those with marital difficulties.

At any one time almost 10 per cent of the general population is suffering from depression, and more than 10 per cent has one or other of the anxiety disorders. Many others have a range of psychological problems and personal difficulties. It is of the greatest importance that treatments of proven effectiveness are developed. However, even when the armoury of therapies is, as it were, full, there remains a very great problem – namely that the delivery of treatment is expensive and the resources are not going to be available evermore. Whilst this shortfall could be met by lots of people helping themselves, commonly the natural inclination to make oneself feel better in the present is to do precisely those things which perpetuate or even exacerbate one's problems. For example, the person with agoraphobia will stay at home to prevent the possibility of an anxiety attack; and the person with bulimia nervosa will avoid eating all potentially fattening foods. Whilst such strategies might resolve some immediate crisis, they leave the underlying problem intact and provide no real help in dealing with future difficulties.

So, there is a twin problem here: although effective treatments have been developed, they are not widely available;

and when people try to help themselves they often make matters worse. In recent years the community of cognitive behavior therapists have responded to this situation. What they have done is to take the principles and techniques of specific cognitive behavior therapies for particular problems and represent them in self-help manuals. These manuals specify a systematic program of treatment which the individual sufferer is advised to work through to overcome their difficulties. In this way, the cognitive behavioral therapeutic techniques of proven value are being made available on the widest possible basis.

Self-help manuals are never going to replace therapists. Many people will need individual treatment from a qualified therapist. It is also the case that, despite the widespread success of cognitive behavioral therapy, some people will not respond to it and will need one of the other treatments available. Nevertheless, although research on the use of cognitive behavioral self-help manuals is at an early stage, the work done to date indicates that for a very great many people such a manual will prove sufficient for them to overcome their problems without professional help.

Many people suffer silently and secretly for years. Sometimes appropriate help is not forthcoming despite their efforts to find it. Sometimes they feel too ashamed or guilty to reveal their problems to anyone. For many of these people the cognitive behavioral self-help manuals will provide a lifeline to recovery and a better future.

Professor Peter Cooper
The University of Reading

Preface

This book is in the form of a self-help program for dealing with problem worries, fears and anxieties. Its aim is twofold: first, to help the reader develop a better understanding of the problem; and then to teach the reader some basic coping skills. Part One explains the origins and development of problem worries, fears and anxieties, while Part Two is a practical, step-by-step guide to overcoming these problems. Part Two is based on a self-help programme which has been developed in clinics and doctors' surgeries over the last ten years, using the comments of clients to adjust and improve it.

The self-help section introduces the coping strategies of:

controlled breathing and applied relaxation to ease physical discomforts;

thought management to combat worrying thoughts;

graded practice and problem-solving to help you face fears;

assertiveness training to assist with interpersonal stresses;

time management to limit the stress caused by procrastination and poor organization;
sleep management to help you get a better night's rest;
and coping in the long term to help you keep up
the good work.

It is a good idea to read the entire guide before embarking
on the programme so that you get an overview – this means
that you can then plan your own program realistically, taking
into account your personal requirements and thus avoiding
disappointment. You can then work through Part Two,
taking a section at a time and rehearsing each technique
thoroughly. You need to be familiar with all the techniques
in the book if you are to be able to judge which suit you,
and the techniques need to be practised if they are to become
second nature to you.

Managing your problems will be achieved through the
investment of time, setting realistic goals for yourself and
gradually building up your self-confidence. Maintaining
your achievements will come through keeping your coping
skills up to scratch and knowing how to learn from
set-backs.

This is not a program that you have to carry out alone,
unless you choose to do so. You can enlist the help of family
and friends, particularly in the practical tasks, and I recom-
mend that you do so. If you decide to do this, encourage
them to read this book so that they might better understand the difficulties that you are trying to overcome and
the ways in which you are tackling your problems. If your
family or friends are going to be able to help you, they also

need to appreciate that anxiety management requires time and careful planning.

There is nothing to lose by working through this book; it will equip you with basic coping skills. However, some readers might find that self-help alone is insufficient to meet their needs, and in these cases the reader is advised to consult a family doctor, medical practitioner or specialist therapist who can offer extra support. If you find that you do need to seek more help, this is not an indication of failure, but a recognition of the complexity of your difficulties.

PART ONE

Understanding Worry, Fear and Anxiety

1

The stress response

Worries, fear and anxieties are common to us all. They are not physically or mentally damaging and, on most occasions, these responses are reasonable or even vital to survival. They are the normal reactions to stress or danger and only become a problem when they are exaggerated or experienced out of context. For example: I hear an approaching bus; I worry that it might hit me; I fear for my life and I experience the sensations of anxiety. This is a perfectly normal, helpful response if I am crossing the road, but an exaggerated and unhelpful reaction if I am resting in the park and the bus is in a nearby lane.

Normal responses to stress

It couldn't have been more idyllic. A peaceful summer's day in the country, just me and my young son. Then I heard the bull and saw that it was running towards us. I felt a whoosh of adrenaline and my heart jumped into my throat. The hair on the back of my neck bristled, my body tensed and all I could think of was my son's safety. I had to get him to safety. I scooped him up and ran. I forgot his toys, I forgot the camera, I was so focused on the gate at the edge of the field and our escape. I don't know where the energy came from but I found the strength to carry him and I was able to get to the gate before the bull reached us. Afterwards, I felt jittery and exhausted but this eased off with time.

Worry, fear and anxiety are crucial to our survival because they prepare us for coping with stress or danger. They trigger the release of a hormone (adrenaline) which promotes physical and mental changes which prepare us for either taking on a challenge or fleeing from a dangerous situation. Once the stress or danger has passed, these temporary changes subside.

Our ancestors were faced with very tangible threats to their safety, such as a wild animal or a hostile neighbour, so for them this *fight-flight* response was highly appropriate. The stresses which we face today tend to be more subtle: delays, ongoing domestic problems, deadlines, job loss. Nonetheless, we experience the same bodily, mental and behavioral changes as did our ancestors.

The bodily changes

. . . I felt a whoosh of adrenaline and my heart jumped into my throat. The hair on the back of my neck bristled, my body tensed . . .

The bodily responses that we are likely to experience include heightened muscular tension, increased breathing rate, raised blood pressure, perspiration and digestive changes.

All of these reactions increase our readiness for action and explain many of the bodily sensations that we associate with anxiety, such as tense muscles, panting, racing heart, sweating, 'butterflies'. This is the ideal state for someone who has to react with a burst of energy: the athlete who is about to run an important race, for example. Without these physical changes, he would be sluggish rather than primed for action.

The psychological changes

. . . all I could think of was my son's safety. I had to get him to safety. I scooped him up and ran. I forgot his toys, I forgot the camera, I was so focused on the gate at the edge of the field and our escape . . .

The psychological changes associated with stress include changes in the way we think, and sometimes in the way we feel, which, again, help us to cope under stress. When faced with danger or stress, our thinking becomes more focused and there can be an improvement in concentration and problem-solving. This is an ideal state of mind for anyone facing a serious challenge – a surgeon carrying out an operation, a stockbroker making a swift decision about an investment, a parent restraining a child who is about to walk into the road. Without the stress response their reactions might be too careless.

We can also experience a range of emotional responses to stress, such as increased irritability or even a sense of well-being. Imagine the stressed father becoming short-tempered with his children, or the executive who becomes exhilarated as she gets closer to meeting her stressful dead-lines, or the excited teenager watching a horror film.

The behavioral changes

. . . I don't know where the energy came from but I found the strength to carry him and I was able to get to the gate before the bull reached us . . .

The behavioral responses to stress or danger are usually forms of escape or vigilance (i.e. flight or fight). If I see a tree branch falling towards me, I get a burst of energy and jump out of the way in order to escape. If I am driving and go into a skid, I become particularly determined to correct this and I find the strength to hold on to the steering wheel. Again, these are vital reactions: without such changes in behavior I would find myself trapped under a branch or caught up in an uncontrolled skid.

Thus, the bodily, mental and behavioral responses to stress are normal, helpful and often vital; and, up to a point, our ability to cope with stress improves as we undergo more stress. This is shown in Figure 1.1. At the bottom of the curve, we are relaxed but physically and mentally ill-equipped to deal with danger because we are not primed for action when we are in this state. As our tension rises, our body and mind become increasingly able to confront stress.

Long-term stress

I used to be positive about myself and had energy and ideas, but I've lost all that since we started to go through

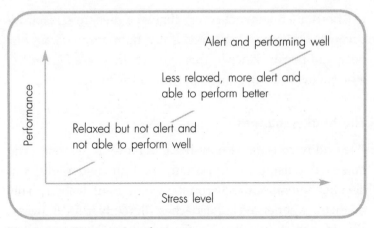

Figure 1.1   Stress and performance

a crisis with the business. Now I really have to push myself to do routine things because I feel so tired and dull. Even when I do get things done, I get no enjoyment from it and so everything feels like a chore. It doesn't end there because I go home worrying about the business and about my performance. I can't get these things out of my mind so I don't even bother to try to be sociable any more. Sometimes I feel quite ill with it all and I haven't slept properly in months. I can't understand how I can push myself and not seem to get anywhere.'

Clearly, the changes brought about in the stress response are helpful in the short term because they prepare our bodies for physical action and focus our minds on the immediate problem. However, they evolved as an immediate and temporary response to stress which was switched off as soon as the danger passed. Problems can arise if these reactions are not switched off, that is, if the stress response becomes chronic or excessive. If this happens, we pass our peak and performance begins to deteriorate: see Figure 1.2, which illustrates the stress-performance curve.

The bodily changes

The bodily sensations now become more unpleasant. The muscular tension, so important for fight and flight, can develop into muscular discomfort throughout the body. This might be experienced as headaches; difficulty in swallowing; shoulder, neck and chest pain; stomach cramps; trembling and weak legs. With prolonged or extreme stress, a person can become aware of the heart pounding and, as blood pressure rises, begin to experience light-headedness, blurred vision, ringing in the ears. As breathing rate increases one might feel dizzy, nauseous and short of breath. If the digestive system is affected by prolonged stress, sickness, diarrhoea and stomach pain can result. Finally, sweating

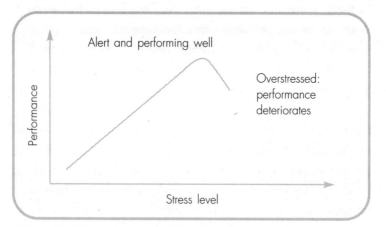

Figure 1.2   The stress–performance curve

can become excessive and, although this is not harmful, it can cause embarrassment.

The psychological changes

The psychological reactions, if sustained, cause thinking to become far too focused on worrying so that a person always fears the worst, worrying that a problem is insoluble and generally thinking negatively. Such negative thinking can form a vicious cycle with the bodily changes during stress if physiological reactions trigger worries such as: 'Pains in my chest. There's something wrong with my heart!' or 'This feeling is unbearable and there's nothing I can do about it.' This will keep stress levels high and prolong the physical discomfort and, therefore, the worrying.

The emotional changes which can occur because of ongoing worry and anxiety are typically those of irritability, constant fearfulness and demoralization. When any of us is feeling like this we find it much more difficult to cope with stress, and when our coping resources are low the stress is much more likely to get on top of us.

The behavioral changes

The changes in behavior, if persistent, can also give rise to difficulties. Constant fidgeting and rushing around becomes exhausting, making one tired and less able to handle stress. Increased comfort eating, smoking or drinking can cause physical and mental problems and take a toll on one's health and sense of well-being. The most common response to fear is running away, or avoiding the situation or object which triggers fear. However, the relief obtained from avoidance is often only temporary and leads to a loss of self-confidence so that the situation soon becomes even more difficult to face.

You can see that the response to stress can itself become distressing. This might be because the physical changes are alarming, or because the worrying and the emotional changes impair one's ability to cope, or because a loss of self-confidence makes it difficult to face fears and overcome them. Whatever the reason, when the natural stress response causes more distress, a cycle has been created which is difficult to

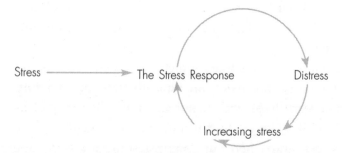

Figure 1.3   The stress–distress cycle

control (see Figure 1.3). This cycle, which maintains the stress response after it has been triggered, is the common factor in all forms of *problem* worry, fear and anxiety.

What triggers the stress response?

The actual trigger for the stress response might be a real or an imagined threat. For example, a man with a snake phobia would experience distress on seeing a real snake or on coming across a picture of a snake. He would have the same response if he *believed* that he had seen a snake or if he *believed* that he was likely to come into contact with a snake in a zoo, for example. A woman who was fearful of public speaking would feel panicky as she stood to give a speech at a wedding, but she might feel just as afraid if she *believed* that she would be asked to stand up and speak without warning.

Whatever the trigger, the keys to persistent problems are the *maintaining cycles* of worry, fear and anxiety. These will be explored in the next chapter.

2

When it becomes a problem

Once I start to worry, I don't seem to be able to stop. Something enters my head and just seems to take over. I get upset and tense when this happens and then I begin to worry that I am doing myself physical harm by being so tense. This sets off another chain of worries and then I get scared that I am losing my mind. I try to avoid things that might set off my anxieties but then I get concerned that I am getting more and more withdrawn. There sometimes doesn't seem to be a way out.

So often a perfectly healthy or normal response to stress develops into a problem because a person gets caught up in a cycle which perpetuates the stress. The cycle can be one which is driven by bodily sensations, by a psychological reaction, by certain behavior or by social circumstances. Sometimes it is a combination of these factors. The first step in breaking the pattern is to distinguish the various cycles that perpetuate your distress.

Bodily maintaining cycles: Reactions to distress

Bodily responses to stress can begin a cycle of distress. Although the physical experience of worry, fear or anxiety is normal, it can be alarming and can lead to greater levels of tension and worry if the reaction is misinterpreted or excessive. The normal, muscular tension of the stress response can be misinterpreted as 'Chest pain: this is a heart attack!', or the respiratory changes might be misconstrued as 'I can't breathe: I'll suffocate!', or the light-headedness of tension might be misunderstood as 'I'm getting dizzy. I'll collapse. I'm having a stroke!' Alternatively, the reaction might simply be 'I can't cope!' Reaching such alarming conclusions would increase anyone's distress

Even though a person might recognize that the muscular pain and difficulties in breathing were simply a response

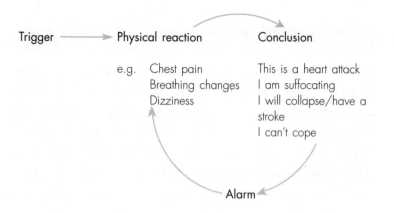

Figure 2.1   How physical reactions maintain stress

to stress, if the bodily reactions are extreme the experience can be uncomfortable and frightening enough to give rise to a fear of the symptoms of anxiety: a fear of fear. Anticipation of this discomfort, the fear of finding oneself in pain and having difficulty breathing, can then produce the stress that triggers the problem.

Bodily reactions to stress can perpetuate problems in other ways. The physical symptoms of shaking, sweating, nausea and faltering voice can indeed impair a person's performance, particularly in public or social settings. An awareness of this can easily undermine the confidence of an anxious person, increase worries about performance and worsen the physical symptoms. Consider the person who is afraid of spilling tea as he carries a cup across a room, or the anxious child who has to recite a poem to his class and is scared that he might falter. In each case the fear of making mistakes could bring about what the individual most fears: trembling to the point of spilling the tea, and becoming inarticulate.

Psychological maintaining cycles: Biased thinking

These are mental and emotional processes which intensify and become distorted as fear levels increase. Anxiety-related problems tend to be associated with the overestimation of danger coupled with an underestimation of coping resources. For example, overestimating the dangers of driving and underestimating one's driving skill would be consistent with a fear of driving; overestimating the likelihood of failing an examination and underestimating one's intellectual ability would give rise to performance fears.

This unbalanced view is unnerving and can further increase distress which, in turn, can enhance *psychological distortion* or *bias* so that the reality of the situation and one's ability to cope recedes further. Imagine that you are running late for an appointment and you can't immediately spot your car keys on the kitchen table. If you weren't under pressure, you would simply scan the room in case you had put them somewhere else; and if you did not see them, you would begin to think of all the other places where you might have left them.

In a state of stress, the importance of the meeting increases: 'This is the one meeting this week that I can't afford to miss!' (overestimating the danger) and the expectation of finding your keys diminishes: 'I'll never find them in time!' (underestimating ability to cope). You become more anxious and your mind goes blank. You can't think where they might be. You begin to predict that you will miss the appointment and your position in the firm will be at risk. The worry makes you careless as you pick up bowls and cushions at random, unable to organize your search. Your tension levels rise further and all you can think about are the disastrous consequences of missing this now *very* important meeting. You are so focused on your escalating fears that you miss the obvious – your partner points out that the keys are in your pocket.

In this example, it is clear that an anxious mind can be a distorting mind, biased towards the negative with thoughts such as: 'I'll never find them!' Such biased thinking is a common response to stress. The most common of the thinking biases are:

- catastrophizing;
- black-and-white thinking;
- exaggerating;
- overgeneralizing;
- ignoring the positive;
- scanning.

While you are reading through the descriptions below, consider how many are typical of you.

Catastrophizing

This is anticipating disaster as the only outcome; anyone who always assumes the worst will experience distress. When catastrophizing, a person would automatically assume that an official envelope must contain a huge tax demand, that a scowl from a colleague indicates absolute hatred, that a tremor in the aircraft is a sign of engine failure, that minor surgery will result in death. Although the images of catastrophizing are dramatic and extreme, the process can take only moments to trigger severe anxiety.

Catastrophizing is particularly associated with physical symptoms: a headache heralds a stroke; chest pain means heart attack; skin tingling or numbness is interpreted as a sign of multiple sclerosis; a lump below the skin surface is believed to be cancer; a sore throat is believed to be the beginning of a bout of influenza that will stop you from completing the work you have lined up and that will mean that you never catch up with yourself and your reputation will be damaged for good!

Black-and-white thinking

This means seeing everything in all-or-nothing terms rather than experiencing more moderate responses: 'I will always feel this badly,' rather than 'I feel bad at the moment but I could get better with help,' or 'Everyone always picks on me,' rather than 'Sometimes I am criticized and sometimes this is unjustified.'

Another common form of black-and-white thinking is expecting perfection in oneself: 'If it isn't perfect, it isn't acceptable.' 'This is not quite right: I have failed.' None of us is perfect, certainly not all of the time. To expect this is to set oneself up for disappointment and further stress.

Exaggerating

This refers to the process of magnifying the negative or frightening aspects of one's experiences. Thinking biases tend to coexist, and exaggeration is often coupled with *overgeneralizing* and then jumping to alarming conclusions. An example of this would be a man who feared redundancy and who subsequently began to note and exaggerate only his mistakes and errors. A minor mistake could trigger the following chain of thought: 'I'll never be able to complete this or any other task [black-and-white thinking, overgeneralization] and the manager will see me as incompetent [jumping to conclusions] and I'll lose my job [catastrophizing].' Of course, this would increase the man's stress and the likelihood of his thinking being biased. The increased stress might also impair his work performance and further fuel his fears.

Ignoring the positive

This is a process of mentally filtering out positive and reassuring facts and events, not noticing compliments, not
acknowledging achievements, not recognizing one's
strengths. The student who ignores a range of good grades
and focuses on a single poor result; the nurse who does
not notice the many 'Thank you's from his patients and
dwells on the fact that one patient has criticized his work;
the teenager who forgets that her peers compliment her
appearance because she is unhappy with the way her hair
looks – all are ignoring the positive. Again, anyone who
fails to recognize his or her good points and personal
strengths will lack self-confidence and therefore cope less
well with stress.

Scanning

Searching for the thing we fear can perpetuate problem
anxiety when it results in unnecessary fear. This can arise
either because it increases the likelihood of seeing, feeling
or hearing something scary, or because one experiences false
alarms. For example, a person who did not fear spiders
would probably walk into a room without noticing cobwebs,
dusty corners or even spiders. However, when the spider-
phobic person entered the same room, not a single web,
corner or crawling creature would go unobserved, thereby
arousing fear. Similarly, someone without health fears could
tolerate aches, pains and minor discomforts without giving
them too much notice, while the person with health fears
would notice exactly the same physical sensations, dwell

on them and start to worry that a serious illness was imminent.

A false alarm for someone with a spider phobia might be mistaking fluff on the carpet for a spider or a crack in the wall for a web, while a frightening misinterpretation for a person with health fears would be finding a perfectly benign swelling and presuming this was a malignancy. Both would trigger unjustified, but very real, sensations of fright.

Mood changes

Finally, the mood changes that are sometimes associated with stress can impair one's ability to cope with stress. The experience of constant anxiety can be demoralizing and promote a hopelessness and misery which then undermine coping. It is therefore important to learn how to catch problem worry, fear and anxiety as early as possible. Irritability, which is often linked with stress, can also fuel anxiety because this mood state can easily impair perform-ance or social functioning and thus promote worries about failure.

Thinking biases aren't all bad; they can stand us in good stead for coping with danger. A person driving along a dark road sees a human-like shape move in front of the car. He thinks: 'A child! I'll kill him!' and he brakes. This is a much safer reaction than his considering: 'I wonder if this is a child, or a shadow, or maybe something else ... [not black-and-white thinking]. If it is a child, I might or I might not be travelling fast enough to knock him over [not catastrophizing]. When I think about it, I have been in situations like this before and it's turned out to be a shadow [*not* overgeneralizing]. And when I look back, I appreciate that I have had very few accidents [*not* ignoring the positive] and probably won't have an accident this evening [*not* jumping to conclusions].' Clearly, if the spectre had been a child, he would have been knocked over by now! Likewise, scanning increases the likelihood of spotting the thing we fear and can be essential in the face of real danger: the frightened soldier who scans for the enemy as he moves through a war zone is more likely to survive than the soldier who does not bother to check for danger; the schoolboy who looks out for traffic before he crosses the road will be safer than the unobservant child.

However, although biases in thinking can be helpful under certain circumstances, this psychological process is unhelpful if it is an habitual way of viewing oneself and the world or if it is too readily provoked.

Behavioral maintaining cycles: The search for comfort

Behavioral problems are largely accounted for by the fact that extreme states of tension can give rise to unhelpful behavior and impair performance. One of the natural reactions to perceived danger is to flee from or avoid it. This is comforting in the short term, and helpful if it removes us from real danger. However, *avoidance* of, and *escape* from, unreal danger maintains fear because it prevents a person from learning to cope. A child who fears going to school and is therefore taught at home never learns that school can be a safe place; a man who avoids flying because he predicts that he will not cope never has the opportunity to learn how to cope; a woman who avoids driving on major roadways never discovers that she has the necessary driving skills to tackle main roads.

Avoidance and escape

Avoidance and escape can take obvious or subtle forms. Obvious avoidance and escape is demonstrated by the person who never goes into a frightening shopping mall or who walks in only to race out again. Subtle avoidance is exhibited by the person who enters the shopping mall, but only when accompanied by a friend or when leaning on a shopping trolley for support or after taking tranquillizers. Subtle escape is shown by the person who goes into the mall but quickly enlists such support. In this way, an anxious person never learns that it is possible to face the fear without help, and so the original fear remains intact.

Another common behavior which can worsen the sensations of anxiety is the use of *stimulants* in response to stress, particularly those which contain caffeine. Lighting up a cigarette, drinking a cup of coffee or tea, or eating a chocolate bar for comfort will encourage the release of adrenaline. This in turn will promote stress symptoms which can then further increase discomfort, trigger worrying thoughts and often impair performance. Turning to alcohol is also counterproductive. Although it is a sedative in the short term, it too becomes a stimulant as it is metabolized. Thus, while the immediate effect might be to help you relax, this is short-lived and using alcohol can actually heighten the feelings of stress. You might have already experienced this on those evenings when you have unwound with a drink or two only to find that you woke in the night and were unable to get back to sleep.

If the use of food, drugs or alcohol develops into a long-term coping strategy the physical changes which result (such as overweight, ill health, addiction) can only worsen stress levels and anxiety. If the use of these substances is also a subtle form of avoidance, this will prevent the user from facing fear and learning how to meet the challenge of difficult situations.

Seeking reassurance

Reassurance seeking also fuels problem worries, fears and anxieties. It is very common to seek out professional or informal opinion when we are worried or afraid, and taking assurance is helpful if we use it to develop better ways to deal with our concerns. However, constantly seeking reassurance is not helpful. It indicates that a person has not accepted the assurance and begun to use it to review the situation, but has taken only temporary relief and soon will have to seek reassurance again. It is rather like the child who gets through the statistics exam by writing formulae on his shirt cuff – he never develops an understanding of statistical analysis and becomes reliant on cheating when faced with an exam or on reference books when faced with a statistical problem.

In the very short term, reassurance does give relief without the pressure of developing better ways of dealing with the problem, but this leaves a person increasingly dependent on seeking more reassurance and less able to face and tackle the real issues. To make matters worse, friends, family and professionals can grow tired of being asked for reassurance, and this can strain relationships and give rise to more stress.

Social maintaining cycles: Unhelpful circumstances

Not all maintaining cycles reflect the response of the individual; sometimes problems are underpinned by *stressful situations* or by the *direct or indirect actions of others*. Situations which can give rise to anxiety and worry include stressful work environments, ongoing domestic problems, long-term unemployment, financial pressures and so on. Clearly, altering one's situation can have a significant impact on stress levels, but we all know that it is not always possible to change one's difficult circumstances. It is therefore all the more important to have a range of stress management skills to help in dealing with the pressure so that it can be kept to a minimum.

The actions of other people can also have a marked impact on an individual's stress levels. These actions can be very obvious or quite subtle. Criticizing, bullying and pressuring are unambiguous sources of stress, which most of us could identify, but some much less obvious actions can give rise to stress, even sometimes those which are well-meaning in origin. These can often go unchecked and will continue to undermine a person's ability to cope. Consider the case of a man with health worries: his difficulties and loss of confidence might be maintained because his wife responds to her husband's repeated pleas for reassurance about his health. Another example of subtle (and well-meaning) maintenance of a problem might be the kindly friend who does an agoraphobic person's shopping, thus allowing her to remain at home. Both contribute to maintaining the problem, even though the motives of the wife and friend are generous.

Breaking the cycles

To sum up, once the stress response has been triggered it can be perpetuated by a maintaining cycle which develops because of bodily, psychological, behavioral or social factors, or a mixture of different elements. You need to reflect on all these areas in order to begin to understand what keeps your problem going. When you can recognize the cycles that maintain your worries, fears and phobias, you can start to think about breaking them. Part Two of this book covers practical ways of doing this. The rest of Part One will be devoted to understanding better why you developed your problems and how different kinds of problems can develop.

3

Who is at risk?

I have always been a worrier. My mother would always warn me about the dangers of germs and we had to scrub up every time we went into her kitchen. Grandfather was just as bad because he always predicted doom and gloom and made us quite frightened. Now I'm just like them! I always see and fear the worst and I'm just as concerned about contamination as mother. I have a stressful job and I don't suppose that helps. I cope by restricting the things I do because so much worries me. This means that I don't have much of a social life and this often gets me down.

Worries, fears and anxieties affect us all differently: some of us are very sensitive to them while others seem more robust. Anyone who experiences problems with fears, phobias and anxieties will ask 'Why me?', and this is an important question to answer if you are to gain long-term control of such problems. Understanding 'Why me?' can put the problems in perspective and also indicate where changes need to be made in your lifestyle, outlook and attitudes. The prevention and management of worries, fears and anxieties depends, in part, on understanding the aspects of your life that might make you prone to such problems, that is, your 'risk factors'.

Broadly speaking, risk factors for the development of anxiety-related problems can be linked with:

- personality type;
- family history;
- life stresses;
- psychological style;
- coping skills and style;
- social support.

Personality type

The significance of personality type in the development of stress-related problems is rather controversial, but many would agree that certain characteristics seem to be linked with anxiety-related problems. In the early 1960s cardiologists identified a 'Type A' personality who seemed to have an increased risk of raised blood pressure and other stress-related problems. 'Type A' individuals were characteristically competitive, ambitious individuals with a tendency to ignore stress symptoms. Also in the 1960s, the label 'neurotic' was used to describe those individuals who had a more easily triggered stress response combined with a slower rate of recovery and who were, therefore, much more vulnerable to developing extreme worries and fears.

A very hopeful finding has been that 'Type A' individuals are able to change their behavior and outlook, and can benefit from this. They can learn to reduce their competitive drive and increase their stress awareness and ability to relax, and thus reduce the stress and health problems which they have previously experienced. So even if you feel that you are 'the worrying type' or have 'always been a worrier', you can anticipate being able to change your outlook and the way you feel in yourself.

Family history

We are all born with certain fears, for example of strangers, heights, snake-like objects, novelty, 'creepy-crawlies', and separation. This is a sound evolutionary development because the infant who recoils from a stranger or a precipice, or who cries for help as a snake or a tarantula crawls towards him, will alert an adult and will therefore survive. In time, with the assurances of adults, the child learns not to over-react to these triggers, although some individuals do carry the fears into adulthood. This suggests that fears can be encoded in our genes, and there is the possibility that fears can be passed on in families.

Studies have shown that anxiety disorders can run in families, although it is difficult to know whether this is because of genetic influence or if it is the result of family members observing each others' behaviour and heeding each others' warnings. A fearful mother can easily communicate her health anxieties to her young daughter; an over-concerned father's constant warning that dogs bite can make his son more likely to develop a dog phobia.

Even though there might be strong trends in families, it

is not impossible to overcome fears or tendencies to worry – even those which have long histories. If you had grown up in a French-speaking family and had only learnt to communicate in French, you would still expect to be able to learn another language if you had to.

Life stresses

These can take the form of distinct stressful events, such as a road accident, a sudden tax demand, or losing a job, and also the form of continuous stresses such as long-term physical illness, chronic financial problems, or fears of redundancy. Since the 1970s stressful life events have been linked with the onset of emotional and psychological problems. Whereas 'loss events' are associated with the development of depression, and hope with the lifting of depression, 'threat events' are linked with the onset of anxiety disorders, and events promoting security are linked with recovery from them. For example, a student would have higher stress levels before and during an examination (the threat event), but a lowering of stress levels when she heard that she had passed them (the security event); or a mother would have heightened anxiety while she waited for her child's X-ray results (threat), but this would fall when she learnt the child had only a minor fracture (security).

A life event does not have to be unpleasant in order to cause stress: adjusting to any change gives rise to stress. Welcome events like marriages, house moves, the birth of a child can be just as stressful as unhappy occasions such as personal injury and job loss. So, if you are to estimate your personal risk of stress-related problems, you need to be aware of the amount of *readjustment* you undergo. Remember that life events often cluster, so that a marriage is likely to be linked with a job change and a house move, or redundancy with financial crisis, for example. This means that the person experiencing these events is even more vulnerable to excess stress.

Nor is it only life events in the present which increase the risk of developing anxiety-related problems. Childhood experiences of danger and insecurity can predispose a person to overestimate danger and underestimate ability to cope, and an adult is more likely to be distressed in response to a life event if that event matches a traumatic event in childhood. For example, a man who had been involved in a serious road accident as a boy would react more markedly to witnessing a car crash in adulthood than a person who had not experienced an earlier, similar trauma; a child who was bitten by a dog would be more wary of one as an adult; a girl who had grown up in a family which suffered severe illness might be more sensitive to health fears as an adult.

Understanding the impact of life events and stresses on one's own difficulties helps to put them into perspective. A man who has a panic attack after his daughter's wedding is not showing signs of weakness or madness. The attack is quite understandable, considering how many stresses are involved in preparing for a wedding and the 'loss' of a daughter. A woman who is beset by worry when her husband is told that he might have mild angina is not reacting outrageously if one realizes that both her parents died of coronary problems when she was young.

Psychological style

Earlier, we saw how thinking biases, such as catastrophizing, jumping to conclusions and ignoring the positive, contribute to the onset and maintenance of worry, fear and anxiety. Anyone with a tendency towards this type of biased thinking is going to be more at risk of developing problems than the person whose outlook is rational or balanced.

It has been established that the way we see ourselves and the world is influenced by our mood. Thus, a businessman whose personal qualities and work situation remain stable can feel more or less vulnerable and perceive the world as more or less threatening depending on his mood. At times when he feels quite happy he might well see himself as masterful in a world of welcome challenges. If he has a personal crisis and is unhappy at home, he can begin to believe that he is a failure in all respects and become fearful of the very same work tasks which he previously welcomed. The person in crisis perceives and remembers with a strong sense of threat which can be powerful in intensifying anxiety. In these states of heightened anxiety, individuals are more likely to be subject to the thinking biases and distortions outlined in the previous chapter, and these in turn will fuel biases in thinking. When this happens, anxiety can become self-perpetuating.

Coping skills and style

The majority of the general population has good coping strategies for managing psychological problems and you have probably developed some good ways of coping yourself. The most common coping methods are trying to keep busy and other forms of distraction, or facing the worry and trying to problem-solve; the least popular methods are using drugs and alcohol. Unfortunately, we all sometimes use unhelpful coping strategies and run the risk of worsening the problem we are trying hard to manage. Perhaps the unhelpful strategies are more readily available (comfort eating or drinking and avoidance, for example) or perhaps we use unhelpful means because no one has encouraged us to develop better techniques.

Part Two of this book is dedicated to helping you to develop a repertoire of constructive strategies so that you will be less likely to rely on stress management techniques that are not going to help you in the long term and which could even make your difficulties worse.

Social support

According to social psychologists, vulnerability to emotional problems increases with reduced levels of social support. Social support can take the form of one or more particularly close and confiding relationships and/or a wide network of supportive contacts, such as workmates, other mothers at playgroup and so on. Vulnerability to psychological problems is particularly marked if a person has no one in whom to confide, and even worse if a person suffers the loss of a best friend and confidant. The greater the social support, the more protected we are against trauma and ongoing stresses, so social support is particularly important at those times of major life events and life crises.

A person with a good support network and a reliable confidant is going to be buffered against crisis. An ideal social support network would be a combination of non-intimate friendships and close friends. Of course, this is not always possible, but remember that simply having one friend in whom to confide helps to protect a person from developing emotional problems in the face of stress. Therefore, one's risk of developing worries, fears and anxieties can be modified by altering one's social situation.

SUMMARY

Typically, a person's vulnerability to anxiety-related problems is determined by a combination of elements rather than a single factor. For example, an obsessive disorder might emerge in a woman with a family predisposition who is now facing a serious life event in the absence of a best friend to confide in. Alternatively, following a minor road accident a man might develop a driving phobia after years of hearing his mother warn him about the dangers of driving and at a time he is taking out his first mortgage.

If you are to be able to answer the question: 'Why me?', you will need to have developed an overview of your personal situation. Figure 5 gives you an idea of the factors you need to consider when appraising your worries and fears, both to see how your current difficulties originated and to understand how they are maintained. You can understand how the problem arose in the first place by examining personal risk factors and social risk factors, and you can explain the persistence of your difficulties by identifying the maintaining cycles which apply to you. By the end of this exercise, you should be able to appreciate

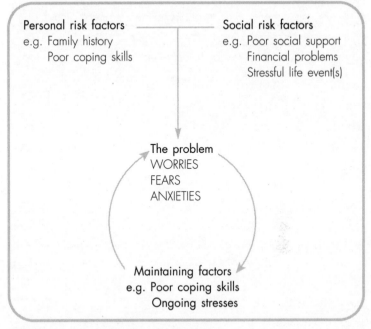

Figure 3.1 Assessing the problem

that your problems do make sense in the context of your history and your current situation.

By now, you will appreciate that it's all too easy to develop problem fears, phobias and anxieties. So it's no surprise to learn that nearly all of us, at some time, will go through a bad patch and find that our levels of fear and anxiety are raised to the point where they cause difficulties. In many cases, this is a temporary dilemma, but the difficulties sometimes persist and a person needs help in reversing the changes.

If you seek help with stress-related problems, you might find your difficulties being labelled or diagnosed by professionals.

This is simply the way in which emotional or psychological problems are classified; these labels direct professionals towards treatment options as well as helping them to describe a problem very succinctly. In the next chapter, we will look at the most common diagnoses of problems associated with worry, fear and anxiety.

4

The forms it can take

Everyone experiences worry, fear and anxiety differently and it is very important that you reflect on and understand what they mean to you personally. Although the experience is a very individual one, professionals have recognized that some fears and anxieties have shared features, and they have attached labels or diagnoses to various different types of problem. You may already have come across some of these. The most commonly used diagnoses are: phobias; panic; generalized anxiety disorder (GAD); obsessive-compulsive disorder (OCD); physical problems and hypochondriasis; 'executive' stress or 'burn-out'; and post-traumatic stress disorder (PTSD).

Phobias

Fears are common, but they become a problem – a phobia – when they are inappropriately intense and/or lead to avoidance and impair one's quality of life. It is important to remember that some intense fears are very healthy – fear of putting one's hand into fire, fear of dogs that are frothing at the mouth and so on – and that some intense fears do not impair the quality of one's life. Phobias concerning climbing ladders might never trouble a person who does not have to do so, while the same fear would be very detrimental to the exterior decorator.

Maintenance of phobias Phobias which do present a problem tend not to diminish over time because the sufferer consistently overestimates the risk to self and practises avoidance. This stops the person from testing out the reality of the fear and also prevents the development of the coping skills which would give him or her some confidence in facing the phobia.

Phobias can be sorted into general categories. The main ones are simple phobia, social phobia and agoraphobia.

Simple phobias

These fears of specific objects or situations are probably the easiest to describe and to understand: fear of wasps, fear of heights, fear of mice, etc. Historically, phobias were classified by the name of the object of fear, which has given rise to some interesting labels, for example:

- apiphobia (fear of bees);
- arachnophobia (fear of spiders);
- brontophobia (fear of thunder);
- emetophobia (fear of vomit);
- haematophobia (fear of blood);
- hydrophobia (fear of water);
- ophidophobia (fear of snakes);
- ornithophobia (fear of birds);
- zoophobia (fear of animals).

Whatever the source of the fear, an object, a *perceived* object, or a situation triggers a powerful anxiety response.

CAT PHOBIA

It might seem silly, and my family certainly thinks it is, but I go to pieces when I see a cat – even if it's only a picture of one. It sets my stomach churning and my heart racing and I think, 'I have just got to get away, I can't handle this!' and then I run.

I have been like this since I was three or four years old and I saw two cats fighting. They were all bloody and then one turned and looked at me. I was terrified. I am very careful not to go into areas where I might see a cat. I don't visit anyone without first checking whether they or their neighbours own a cat. I don't browse in card shops – do you realize how many greeting cards have cats on them? I'm glad that I'm a man and I get sent ships and trains at birthdays! Although I'm joking a bit now, it's no joke if I see a cat, or if I think I've seen a cat. It really affects my day-to-day life and I am restricted in what I can do and where I can go. It's getting worse, rather than better as time goes on.

VOMIT PHOBIA

My husband is getting so tired of us having to take taxis home from local parties and clubs because I can't face walking down our main street. There are so many places where people can get drunk and might vomit, that I can't risk it. If my husband is really firm and insists that we walk home, I make him walk through back streets so as not to encounter someone being sick. Also, I won't visit anyone who is ill and I don't go into work if there is a stomach bug going around. If I discover that someone I know is sick, I worry about it for days.

I've never been comfortable around sickness, but I've only been scared of it since 1990, when I was coming around from an anaesthetic (after I had had my hysterectomy) and I heard the woman in the next hospital bed vomiting all through the night. It was awful. I started to feel nauseous and I began to retch so hard that I was convinced that I was going to die. It was one of the worst nights of my life and I made the hospital staff find me a side room for the rest of my stay. The thought of that time makes me feel panicky and I can feel the nausea come over me. I'd rather not even think about it and I certainly never want to go into hospital again.

Social phobias

Social phobias are different from the very specific, simple phobias in that a person fears a *range* of situations where s/he might be exposed to evaluation – public speaking, for example. Typically, this person predicts and fears negative evaluation. This fear can then undermine that person's performance and this feeds into a cycle of worry.

PUBLIC SPEAKING

The larger the gathering, the worse it is. Ever since I forgot my lines in a school play and everyone laughed, I have been terrified of public speaking. I know it seems ridiculous – I was an eight-year-old schoolgirl then and I am a university lecturer now – but I still feel just as frightened as I did at school. I get clammy hands and I feel my throat tighten and my mind often goes blank or is beset by worries. I worry that I am making a fool of myself or that the audience will think that I'm stupid. I cope by taking tutorials rather than lectures and swallowing the odd Valium. Sadly, it is just impossible for me to present academic papers and my career is suffering, which makes me very nervous. I'm OK at parties because I just merge with the crowd – but I won't play party games because I feel so vulnerable and scared if I'm being watched.

SOCIALIZING

I was once quite outgoing and thought that I was confident. That all changed with my first pregnancy. I put on a lot of weight – much more than I should have, but I didn't mind because I was pleased about the baby and I thought that the weight would disappear after the birth. Partly because I was so huge, we did not socialize much in the late stages of the pregnancy – I just didn't have the energy or the inclination to go out. We did go to a family wedding and I remember finding it quite hard work to mix and chat – but I decided that this was because I was tired.

After my daughter was born, I was overweight, a bit depressed and very tired. I no longer felt confident in myself and I had the most unpleasant time at the baby's baptism. I couldn't find it in me to be cheerful and then I overheard someone say: 'What has happened to Stella, she used to be so lively and attractive?' That just crushed any confidence that I had left and I wouldn't go out for weeks. I was so miserable that I couldn't get rid of the weight and that made me feel worse about meeting others. Now my little girl is five, I am still overweight and I still can't face going to social events unless I have some false courage in the form of a drink or a Valium. I do make myself attend my daughter's school events but I dread them and I keep myself to myself once I'm there. When I can, I persuade my husband to go instead of me.

Agoraphobia

Agoraphobia is not simply a fear of open spaces; it is the fear of leaving a place of safety, such as the home or a car or the doctor's surgery, or a combination of safe places. The fear usually reflects an expectation that something terrible will happen to the individual or to loved ones or to property. Agoraphobia is often associated with panic attacks (see the next section) because the fear response is very powerful.

I have not been out of the house for six months, I did go to see my doctor at Christmas, but I got into such a state that I nearly collapsed and now I get him to see me here. I feel safe here and I don't get the awful feelings, but I'm not even relaxed at home if I know a stranger is visiting. I often have a drink to calm me if the paperboy is coming to collect the paper money or the gas man is coming to read the meter. Sometimes, though, I just refuse to answer the door.

I was always a bit nervous about going out and about and gradually, I went to fewer and fewer places on my own and I began to rely more and more on a glass or two of sherry to give me Dutch courage. A year ago I was able to use the corner shop and to get round the block to see my sister but I can't do that now – even with the sherry. Just talking about it makes me feel wobbly and breathless. I try not to think about the awful feelings I get – thinking about them makes me feel almost as bad as going out does. Sometimes I wonder if I'm going mad. My sister is very helpful, though – she does my shopping and visits me nearly every day.

Panic

The term 'panic attack' describes intense feelings of apprehension or impending disaster coupled with a very powerful physical reaction. Sufferers sometimes find themselves fighting for breath, experiencing chest pains, unable to see clearly and feeling very frightened. The onset of a panic attack is rapid and bodily sensations are very marked, especially if a person overbreathes. Overbreathing, or hyperventilation, is a common reaction during panic and it produces even more distressing physical symptoms, such as dizziness, tingling beneath the skin, muscle pain and ringing in the ears. There can be a wide range of triggers for a panic attack, for example, being faced with a phobia and not feeling able to cope; chest pain misconstrued as a heart attack; or dizziness misinterpreted as an impending stroke.

Maintenance of panic   Panic frequently occurs in combination with other anxiety disorders and is often fuelled by an individual's tendency to jump to frightening conclusions: 'I can't cope!', 'I am dying!' Panic tends to be maintained by misinterpreting symptoms, overestimating danger, anticipating danger, overbreathing and avoidance.

> *I will never forget the first time I had a panic attack – I thought I was dying! I was working on a stressful project and had got really hyped up on black coffee and very little else that day. By the evening, I was running late and knew that I'd have to rush to get to Bobbie's on time. Of course, the traffic was bad and in the back of the taxi I found myself getting more stressed and then I became hot and dizzy and I could hardly breathe. Somehow I paid the driver, but in the apartment I seemed to lose all control. I was sweating, gasping for breath, I had pains in my chest and my vision was getting dim. I couldn't hear what Bobbie was saying because of a ringing in my ears, but she had called a doctor because we both thought that I was having a heart attack. The doctor said that I had had a panic attack and that it was probably caused by the day's stress. This should have reassured me – and it did for*

a day or two – but then I had another and, again, I couldn't get in control of the situation. Although I tell myself that these are not heart attacks and that they cannot harm me, I am now so frightened of the experience that I'm always worried and I avoid places where I've had them.

Generalized anxiety disorder

Generalized anxiety disorder (GAD) is the label used to describe persistent, pervasive feelings of anxiety which give rise to what seems like constant bodily and mental discomfort. Those suffering from GAD explain . . . 'I never seem to be free of worry' or 'I can never relax, something is always troubling me. I am constantly on edge.' They will often describe periods of intensification of anxiety and often state that these occur 'out of the blue'. Such chronic worry is both physically and emotionally draining.

Maintenance of GAD It is generally thought that GAD is underpinned by many worries or the misinterpretation of a wide range of situations as threatening. This collection of fears needs to be teased out in treatment and each tackled individually.

I always worry and I never relax nowadays. There is never a moment when I am free of aches and tension and my mind is almost always focused on worries. It makes me so tired and irritable and I have not been able to sleep or work properly and have not felt well in months.

It seems to have crept up on me over the last year or two. Others have always said that I was highly strung but this was never a problem – I just seemed to have more 'nervous energy' than most and I used this to my advantage. If anything, I should be more relaxed now that the children have gone to university, the recession seems to be coming to an end and my husband and I have more time to spend together. Instead, I'm even more edgy than usual – perhaps I haven't got enough to occupy my mind, I don't know.

I saw my doctor who said that I should join a yoga class and learn to unwind – I tried but I found it impossible to concentrate and I ended up getting more and more irritable! Now I try to cope by keeping busy in the shop, but this isn't easy because I am so tired that I can't seem to concentrate so I make silly mistakes and that stresses me and winds me up even more. I feel so hopeless that I just can't imagine when this is going to end.

Obsessive-compulsive disorder

Obsessive-compulsive disorder (OCD) describes a compulsion to carry out particular acts or to dwell on certain mental images or thoughts in order to feel at ease. For example, a person might feel compelled to wash his hands repeatedly or to check over and over again that switches are turned off; another person might experience OCD as the compulsion to dwell on a mental image of her family being safe and well or to repeat specific and reassuring phrases. There is a chain of reactions in OCD: first, a *perceived* threat triggers a worrying thought (or image), and this in turn compels the sufferer to engage in a reassuring mental or physical activity.

Some sufferers describe OCD as the most embarrassing of the anxiety disorders and many individuals who are troubled by it will never disclose their problem; yet responding to a worrying thought or image is a useful response if it is not exaggerated. Imagine that you are leaving your house and you think: 'Did I switch off the gas fire? It would be dangerous to leave it on all day.' This might then concern you enough to go back and check. Consider the woman who reads an article about cervical cancer which triggers the worrying thought 'I could be at risk' and prompts her to get a health check. Think of the father who, when driving home, sees a cyclist without lights being knocked off her bicycle: this triggers an unpleasant image of his own children being injured and prompts him to check that they have working lights when they go out at night. Each of these reactions is useful but would present a problem if you felt compelled to return several times to check the fire, or experienced recurrent health fears and made repeated appointments with the doctor, or were constantly beset by frightening images of your children and became overprotective to reassure yourself.

Maintenance of OCD   Coping with OCD most often takes the form of avoidance, which then perpetuates the problem: for example, returning to the house twenty times to avoid the discomfort of worrying about a fire; repeated reassurance-seeking from the doctor to avoid harbouring health fears; restricting the behavior of children to avoid worrying about their welfare. Thus, the sufferer never learns that the fears are unfounded or bearable and they remain intact.

OCD and health worries

I suppose that I have two compulsive problems: I worry that I could be contaminated by germs in my environ- ment and so I wash a lot to avoid this. I also worry about my family's health and so I've stopped reading papers or watching TV programmes that could set off my worries. If I start to worry, my mind gets filled with the most awful images of death and I have to think about everyone I love while saying: 'You're OK.' If I don't do this, or if I do it in the wrong sequence, I can't get rid of the worries. The images stay in my mind and I feel so distressed that I just can't bear it.

I know that this must sound really weird, and I would think it was weird if I didn't know how easy it is to get caught up in these worries which will only go away if I wash or go through my 'You're OK' ritual. I can't actu- ally remember a time when I didn't think like this, although there have been times in my life where it's hardly been a problem, and times when it's dominated my days. The only way I know how to cope is to try to avoid situations which make me feel contaminated or worried about death. That's why I don't watch TV programmes about health issues, nor do I read that sort of article in the newspaper. If someone starts to talk about illness, I often make an excuse to walk away, and if I can't do this, than I have to wash or to go through my 'You're OK' ritual as soon as I can. Sometimes I can't get away to do this and I feel absolutely terrified for hours.

OCD and safety worries

I never worried much until I was in the army. We saw so many awful things and witnessed so many personal disasters that I think that we all became a bit superstitious about things. We would take 'lucky' items into dangerous situations and even the strongest of us could get upset if he couldn't find his lucky charm. I suppose that we had such little control over what happened to us that we did these simple things to try to feel more in control. I can remember that I did get rather obsessional about safety checks – something that I could have control over – and I would double and triple check my equipment so that I took no extra risks. Once I left the army, I gradually gave up a lot of my obsessive checking and, although my wife has always commented on my attention to safety, I've never had a problem with it. That is until six months ago.

It was around that time that I set a retirement date and was planning all sorts of changes in my life. Knowing that I only had another year with the firm, my boss suddenly promoted me to an executive position with a lot more responsibility – particularly financial. He said that he wanted to send me off with a good bonus and a recognition of my abilities. That was an admirable gesture but one which increased my stress levels. I found myself worrying more and more about the safety of the office. I would travel home wondering if I had locked my office, locked the safe, set the burglar alarm, and so on. Very soon I could picture the safe being broken into because of my negligence and then I saw myself shamed in front of the man who had trusted me with this extra responsibility. By now I was so worried that I would return to the office time after time to check the safe, to check my office and to check the alarm. I could do this as many as twenty times and I began getting home later and later and more and more upset. My wife says that she can't stand much more of this.

Physical problems and hypochondriasis

By now, it will be clear that the stress response is a very physical reaction and, if it is prolonged, can become uncomfortable and give rise to physical problems.

Physical problems

Sometimes these are the first indication that a person is overstressed. Typical physical symptoms are difficulty in sleeping, stomach and digestive troubles, headaches, raised blood pressure, worsening asthma, difficulty in swallowing, nausea and sickness, diarrhoea.

Maintenance of physical problems   Stress can both cause and maintain these conditions. A child might have nausea and diarrhoea because pressures at school cause her stress, and this physical response could then cause her additional worry which would maintain the stress and sickness. A man might discover that he has developed high blood pressure and be so concerned by this that his anxiety levels increase and further elevate his blood pressure.

SLEEP PROBLEMS

It's all very well for my doctor to say, 'Just relax and then you'll find that you sleep better,' but she's not the one who is tossing and turning for hours, worrying that another night of poor sleep is going to make the next day hell. I'm a teacher and I find it impossible to control a classroom full of children if I am feeling exhausted, and that's how I feel every day. I do avoid coffee now but it doesn't help much because I have reached the point where I am on edge all of the time. I dread going to bed because I know I won't sleep properly and then I can predict that I won't be able to cope well the next day at school. Knowing this winds me up so much that the last thing I'm able to do is relax!

GASTRIC PROBLEMS

I get so irritated with my sister who keeps saying: 'It's all in your mind.' When I go on a car journey, I assure you that it's all in my stomach! While I'm at home I feel well enough – unless I know that I have to go out later and then I can get into a bit of a state and have to go to the lavatory two or three times – but, as a rule, I am only poorly on journeys. That's why I rarely go anywhere now. I stopped using public transport ages ago because I can't stop to get out. I don't visit my sister, who lives thirty miles away, and I rely on the telephone much more now. Luckily, most of my family members live close by and they seem happy to drop in on me.

If I have to make a trip, I will take some calming tablets that the doctor gave me. They make it possible for me to get to and from the clinic where they're giving me more tests to try to sort out my problem.

Hypochondriasis

This term specifically describes a stress-related problem where there is distress in response to *perceived* symptoms. This is often associated with extra sensitivity to normal bodily sensations and/or a preoccupation with the fear of catching a serious disease.

Maintenance of hypochondriasis Hypochondriacal worries are so strong that they tend to be resistant to reassurance, although the sufferer often seeks repeated reassurances. This is not helpful because reassurance prevents that person from learning to reassure him/herself and to overcome the health fears. Hypochondriasis is also maintained by repeated checking for signs of illness. We all have bodily discomforts which are benign and we all have occasional swellings and skin discolorations. Therefore, anyone who looks for these will find them and can be alarmed by the discovery. If a person goes on to prod and rub swellings or spots, they get worse and serve to frighten that person even more.

I have always been concerned about my health, but I was never really worried until a year ago when I heard that awful story about the young mother who suddenly died of leukaemia, leaving three small children. I've got three children so the story really hit home and that day I began checking for swellings and bruises. I was soon carrying out a full body check three times a day and calling in to see my doctor every few days. He kept telling me that there was nothing to worry about and that I had probably caused small bruises by prodding my body so much. I'd feel OK for a while but my doubts always returned and my fears became stronger.

Now, I also get my husband to check my body morning and evening so that I can feel confident that I haven't missed anything. He's getting fed up with this and we row a lot and this just makes me worse. Recently, my doctor has told me that he doesn't want to have to see me nearly every day at the surgery and I am finding it so hard not to go – sometimes I pretend that one of the children is sick and use that as an excuse to get an appointment. The strange thing is, the more checking I do, the more worried I get but, as I see it, you can never be sure, can you?

Burn-out

This is a recently coined term which is used to describe a reaction to constant stress which tends to go unnoticed until the sufferer, or someone close, realizes that s/he is not coping. The long-term stress can be 'positive', such as overwork, pressured deadlines or impossible targets, or 'negative', such as job boredom, lack of autonomy or frustration. Whatever the origin, the symptoms are similar to those in other stress-related disorders, but tend to be more marked because the stress is ignored or dismissed until it has become quite severe and has reached levels which interfere with a person's work performance and sense of well-being.

Maintenance of excess stress   The stress may be ignored through habit, as with the overworked mother who never pauses to consider the pressure that she is under; or because stress is construed as 'excitement', as with the enthusiastic stockbroker who says that he 'lives on adrenaline' and enjoys it; or because an individual's drive overrides the awareness of stress, as with the ambitious person who is determined to succeed at all costs; or simply because a person can't say, or fears saying, 'No' and thus ends up taking on too much work and becoming overburdened.

Looking back, all the signs were there but I never took any notice. I had always wanted to be a nurse and I was ambitious for myself and concerned about my patients. So I never stopped to look at how hard I was working. Actually, it is difficult to slow down in my job – the culture of an emergency ward is one of self-sacrifice and hard work. I began to get digestive problems, but I simply took antacids and when I was diagnosed as having irritable bowel syndrome, I thought it was a nuisance but I did not realize that it was a warning sign. I began to get more and more run down and told myself that this is what happens in the winter and that we still have to run the service. I was losing weight, feeling exhausted and getting so irritable that some of my staff were obviously giving me a wide berth.

The most frightening part of my experience was that I began to make mistakes – often really stupid ones that I wouldn't expect of a student. Fortunately, I had not made many before my line manager insisted that I was signed off work to recover from stress. At the time I was shocked and it took a while to sink in but now I recognize that it was the best thing that could have happened and I thank goodness the decision hadn't been left to me – I don't think that I would have realized that I was suffering from burn-out until I had made far too many mistakes.

Post-traumatic stress disorder

Post-traumatic stress disorder (PTSD) is a stress reaction which follows unusually traumatic events such as a road traffic accident, rape, or witnessing a major disaster. The first studies of PTSD involved soldiers who had been engaged in military combat and who showed similar patterns of extreme stress reactions. The main features, which were usually accompanied by classic symptoms of anxiety, were recurrent, vivid memories or dreams of the event. In some cases this was associated with emotional intensity, such as a much greater sensitivity to fright or more than usual tearfulness. Sometimes the post-traumatic reaction was one of emotional numbing, that is, feeling very little or having blunted or deadened emotions. This reaction has proved to be a familiar consequence of a range of traumatic events, and it reflects a natural process of recovery which can take a few months to resolve.

Maintenance of PTSD   Although the stress response associated with trauma usually fades without intervention, for some it presents a longer-term problem, particularly if the traumatized person avoids persons, places or issues which restimulate memories of the event. This avoidance can take behavioral or mental forms: either way, it serves to maintain the symptoms of PTSD. Although it can be very distressing, facing the memories of trauma seems to be one of the most effective ways of dealing with PTSD.

After the car crash, I started to have dreams about it. I expected these to go away within a few days, but they were persistent and so vivid that I would wake up really believing that I had just relived the accident. I know, from talking to others, that this is a common reaction, but my terrifying dreams persisted for weeks and weeks and they were affecting my sleep and my ability to work the next day. Eventually, the doctor gave me some sleeping tablets to help me cope with this.

Although I was then less bothered by the dreams I still could not bring myself to go back to the junction where the accident had happened, nor could I bring myself to drive the car again. I thought that I'd soon get over my fear of driving and of that junction, but I found that it got worse rather than better and I became very dependent on my wife to do the driving and to plan routes which didn't take in that junction. If we did get close to the scene of the accident, I would start to have really vivid memories – like a flashback of the original scene. This upset me so much that my wife soon learnt lots of alternative routes and we now stick to them. She's been so understanding about this and she has really put herself out to help. Although it's now been six months since the crash, I still don't feel confident that I will be able to drive again and being so restricted in my freedom to travel is affecting my work.

Despite the variation in the types of problems experienced related to worry, fear and anxiety, and the different labels applied to them, there are psychological methods of management which can give relief in all of these cases. These techniques are described in detail in Part Two of this book.

5

Managing problems

> *I have suffered with my nerves for years and I have always managed by taking the odd tranquillizer. I always take one before I go to a social event or if I have to visit the doctor or dentist. Although this has worked for me, I do worry that I might be dependent on the tablets. I did get into a terrible state on holiday when I ran out and it ruined the holiday for everyone. After that, my husband said that I should try to cope without them but I haven't the courage.*

Traditionally, the options for managing worries, fears and anxieties have been psychological methods and/or medication. Although medication was very popular in the 1970s and early 1980s, more recently psychological methods have been gaining popularity. Tranquillizers are not necessarily a bad thing as long as they are used under the advice of a doctor. In fact, tranquillizers might be invaluable for helping someone through a crisis; but their long-term use is generally considered to be unhelpful.

There are several strong arguments for adopting a psychological rather than a pharmacological or drug-based approach: first, there is evidence that drugs promote dependency while being no more effective than psychological management; secondly, drugs can provide a means of subtle avoidance for the user who can then become psychologically dependent on medication; thirdly, there is also the possibility that tranquillizers will simply mask symptoms of worry, fear and anxiety but will not address the root of the problem, which may then remain a source of vulnerability to stress; finally, medication can give rise to unpleasant side-effects which might even worsen the anxieties of someone who is very sensitive to bodily changes.

On the positive side, there is increasing evidence that those suffering from anxiety-related difficulties can benefit from self-help – as long as the self-help program is organized in a way that helps sufferers to pace themselves realistically and as long as the techniques in that program are very well rehearsed. Part Two of this book presents a recovery program in the form of a range of coping strategies which can help modify the physical, psychological and behavioral symptoms associated with problem anxiety. Anyone planning to reduce her or his use of tranquillizers should anticipate having to invest time in learning and practising the self-help strategies.

Coming off tranquillizers

Some of those reading this book will already be using tranquillizers which they are hoping to be able to give up. Learning self-help skills to replace the medication is the surest way of being able to come off tranquillizers, but it is possible that the process will be made more difficult by withdrawal symptoms. Not everyone experiences these, so don't *anticipate* suffering as you cut down on the tranquillizers. However, you should always seek the advice of your doctor before modifying your medication and you should tell him or her if you are experiencing discomfort. Common withdrawal symptoms to be aware of are:

- feelings of anxiety;
- loss of concentration, poor memory;
- agitation, restlessness;
- stomach upsets;
- oversensitivity;
- feelings of unreality;
- physical tensions and pains;
- appetite changes;
- difficulty sleeping.

If you are one of those who does experience symptoms of withdrawal, reassure yourself that they are temporary and that your body and mind will adjust to not using medication to deal with your fears and worries. When you do reduce your medication, try not to substitute alcohol or food or smoking for comfort, as these can cause you further problems to worry about. Instead, use the self-help strategies in Part Two of this book.

SUMMARY

1 Worry, fear and anxiety are normal and healthy responses to stress. They are very necessary for our survival and only become a problem when they are exaggerated and cycles of distress develop.

2 These cycles are maintained by physical, psychological, behavioral and social factors, but you can learn to break these cycles and control your distress.

3 In order to do this, you must understand your own worries, fears and anxieties in terms of your personal and social risk factors, and the cycles that perpetuate your difficulties.

PART TWO

Managing Worries, Fears and Anxieties

6

What can I do?

*I had given up thinking that things could be different.
My old doctor had always given me tablets to help me
deal with difficult situations. When a new doctor told
me that I could manage without them, I thought that
she did not realize what she was asking. She explained
that, over time, I could develop ways of managing my
distress for myself and then I could cut down on my
pills. It didn't happen overnight but I did manage to
learn how to deal with stress by myself. That boosted
my self-confidence and then it became even easier to
cope. I felt so much better in myself for not having
to turn to drugs and much more able to take on new
challenges.*

Strategies for coping

In Part One of this book, we established that worry, fear
and anxiety are common and crucial to survival, but that
they can develop into problems when cycles of distress
become established. You can learn to break these cycles by

developing practical ways of overcoming the unpleasant symptoms. There is a range of coping strategies that can help you to modify the bodily, psychological and the behavioral responses associated with problem worry, fear and anxiety, and these will be described in detail in the chapters that follow in Part Two of this book. In summary, you will be introduced to:

- *stress awareness training;*
- *techniques for the management of bodily sensations:*
  - controlled breathing;
  - applied relaxation;
- *techniques for managing the psychological symptoms:*
  - distraction;
  - thought challenging;
- *techniques for dealing with problem behavior:*
  - graded exposure to fears;
  - problem-solving strategies;
  - assertiveness training;
  - time management;
  - sleep management;
- *techniques for coping in the long term:*
  - blueprinting;
  - coping with set-backs.

By using these approaches, you can often bring your problems under control. However, you should remember that coping techniques rarely come naturally and that you need to think of them as *skills* which will only be learned through regular practice. The process of developing these skills is rather like learning to play a musical instrument or to master a new language: if you want to learn how to do it properly, you have to find time to practise. With practice, you will find that you develop effective coping techniques to use whenever you are under stress or anxious. You will then be able to cope with the unpleasant feelings and thoughts that you have associated with stress and this will allow you to face a range of situations that were once very difficult for you.

Some of the strategies you will read about in Part Two of this book may seem familiar, as they could be similar to coping techniques that you have tried already. If certain techniques do seem very like ones that you have used in the past, don't dismiss them straight away as redundant or unhelpful. Instead, read through the sections carefully and check that you have been using the technique properly. If a particular technique was not helpful to you in the past, also consider whether or not you have been practising enough for you to become proficient at putting it into action.

Some of the coping techniques laid out in Part Two will be quite new to you. Don't be put off by novelty, as some of these might prove to be your best coping strategies. However, do recognize that the unfamiliar strategies are likely to need extra attention and practice.

When you have taken yourself through the *entire* program, you will discover which techniques, or combinations of techniques, suit you best; these will form your 'first aid kit' for coping. Each person's 'kit' will be different and it is important that you tailor yours to meet your needs. Thereafter, you can relax in the knowledge that you are carrying around with you effective ways of dealing with worries, fears and anxieties so that you can simply get on with your life.

Choosing your strategies for coping

You cannot choose the appropriate strategies for dealing with your difficulties until you have reviewed your own personal experience of worry, fear and anxiety. You also need to put this in the context of what is feasible for you: you can't plan to overcome your fear of flying by taking flying lessons unless you have the finances and freedom to do so; you can't anticipate relaxing at an expensive gym if you have three small children at home and no money; but you *can* make plans which involve the support of others if you have helpful family and friends, and you *can* make plans that impinge on your daily work if you have sympathetic employers. You will discover more about keeping diaries to identify your personal needs and resources in the next chapter.

As a general guide, look for coping strategies that 'match' the problems you have. For example, if you suffer from the physical discomfort of stress, make sure that controlled breathing and relaxation (Part Two, chapters 3 and 4) are on your skills list. If, on the other hand, you are more bothered by constant worries and nagging fears, invest extra time in learning distraction techniques (Part Two, chapter 5) and how to challenge worrying thoughts (Part Two, chapter 6). The best way to match strategies to your needs

will be covered in more detail in the next chapter, after you
have had an opportunity to keep some records of your
difficulties.

Coping alone or with the help of others?

Although this is a self-help guide to managing your worries,
fears and anxieties, you can enlist the support of others if
doing so will improve your stress management. Partners,
family and friends can be very helpful as allies in coping,
as can professionals such as counsellors and medical practitioners. It is worth spending some time reflecting on what
would be most helpful to you: perhaps it would be a
partner's company when you are learning to relax, or a
friend's support as you try the exercise of facing your fears,
or your doctor's help in reducing your medication. If you
plan ahead with your needs in mind, you will have a
greater chance of being successful in your battle against
worries, fears and anxieties.

What to expect from the self-help program

Many sufferers from worry, fear and anxiety have already
benefited from the self-help plan in this book. It is important, however, to recognize that some individuals will gain
relief from using the self-help program but might not feel
that they have *taken control* of the problem. For example, a
person with OCD might well learn to relax, and will gain
physical relief from this, but might not be able to resist the
impulses to check without the help of another person;

someone with GAD might learn to sleep better and derive benefit from this, but she might not be able to dismiss her daytime worries without the guidance of a therapist. Although these individuals would need some extra support from a friend, a general counsellor or a specialist therapist, they could still gain much benefit from following the program – as long as they recognized the need to seek additional help.

Nonetheless, the self-help approach is an excellent first step. Many do benefit from this program and familiarity with the techniques described here will be fundamental to further therapy. If you find that you are one of those people who requires more support, don't be dismayed; simply contact a professional who can advise you where to go for help.

SUMMARY

1 You can gain relief from problem worry, fear and anxiety by developing techniques which will enable you to become aware of stress and then to deal with the bodily sensations, the psychological symptoms and the problem behavior. You will also need to learn strategies for coping in the long term.

2 By doing this you can learn to break the cycles that maintain your problems and you might well find that you can control your anxieties completely.

3 However, you do not have to do this alone. You can use friends and professionals for extra support. Sometimes this might even be necessary if you are to learn to take full control of your problem.

7

Awareness training and self-monitoring

For a long time, I thought that my panic came out of the blue. This made me even more frightened because I felt out of control. Then I started to keep a diary of my panicky feelings and, to my surprise, I saw a pattern. This made me feel less helpless and I started to reorganize my life to minimize the panics. For example, I got the feelings if I hadn't eaten for hours, so I began to carry snacks in my briefcase; I felt panicky when I had to see my boss, so I attended an assertiveness training class to help me feel more confident around her. I took control again.

Getting to know your worries, fears and anxieties

The experience of worry, fear and anxiety is different for each of us. We do not all experience the same bodily sensations, each of us has our own worrying thoughts, we each behave differently, and the triggers for anxieties vary from person to person. Before you can begin to learn how to manage the problem you must really understand that problem. You can do this quite easily by keeping a record

Diary 1 Logging Stress reactions

Monitor your stress levels each day, noting when you feel particularly worried, frightened or anxious. Use the diary as near to the time of distress as possible as it is easy to forget the details later. Record the occasion and rate the severity of your feelings (1–10). Where you can, note what triggered the stress – thoughts, images, feelings, events, for example. Also, record how you tried to cope, and afterwards, rerate your distress levels.

Rate your distress on the following scale:

1	2	3	4	5	6	7	8	9	10

No distress, calm   Moderate distress   Absolute panic

Date, time	What was the occasion?	Rating	What brought it on?	How did you try to cope?	Rerating

of the times when you are particularly worried, fearful or anxious and then noting your physical feelings, your thoughts and what you do in response to this distress.

Diary 1 is a typical record for logging stress reactions which will help you to structure your record keeping. You will see that, as well as having columns for noting the onset and the experience of stress, there are two columns ('Rating' and 'Rerating') for rating the level of your discomfort from 'Wholly calm' (1) to 'The worst possible reaction' (10), and a column for 'What did you do?' This is because it is useful to differentiate levels of distress in different situations, and also to note what happens to your distress levels after you have tried to cope. You need to know what coping strategies work for you (i.e. reduce your distress) and what strategies do not (i.e. increase your distress).

If you keep a note of your stress for one or two weeks (you'll find extra diary sheets at the end of the book) and then look back over your entries, you should find that you can answer the questions:

- What things or situations trigger *my* distress?
- What are *my* bodily feelings and *my* thoughts when I am distressed?
- What differing levels of distress do different situations cause?
- What do *I* tend to do when I am distressed?
- What helps *me* best to cope with my distress?

Diary 1(a): Dog Phobia

Monitor your stress levels each day, noting when you feel particularly worried, frightened or anxious. Use the diary as near to the time of distress as possible as it is easy to forget the details later. Record the occasion and rate the severity of your feelings (1–10). Where you can, note what triggered the stress – thoughts, images, feelings, events, for example. Also, record how you tried to cope, and afterwards, rerate your distress levels.

Rate your distress on the following scale:

1	2	3	4	5	6	7	8	9	10
No distress, calm				Moderate distress					Absolute panic

Date, time	What was the occasion?	Rating	What brought it on?	How did you try to cope?	Rerating
Saturday 8.30 am	Waiting for Jim and Sue to arrive for our trip and for a drink	8	Worry that I'd see a dog at the bar and I'd go to pieces	1. Tried to do something else: read a magazine 2. Tried something more distracting: rang Mary to talk about work	6 4
1.00 pm	In their car, on way to the bar	8	Ditto	Kept talking to Sue to take my mind off the worries	6
1.20 pm	Sitting outside bar waiting for Jim to bring over the drinks	10	I saw a shape in the parkland – I was sure it was a dog – probably a German Shepherd	1. Screamed. Then Sue told me that it was a small deer, not a dog 2. Drank 2 glasses of wine quickly! 3. Went *inside* bar.	8 4 3
3.00 pm	At home, alone. The alcohol is wearing off.	7	Remembering the stress and the fright of today	Tried to relax in the garden with classical music on my personal stereo	2

Diary 1(b): Social Anxiety

Monitor your stress levels each day, noting when you feel particularly worried, frightened or anxious. Use the diary as near to the time of distress as possible as it is easy to forget the details later. Record the occasion and rate the severity of your feelings (1–10). Where you can, note what triggered the stress – thoughts, images, feelings, events, for example. Also, record how you tried to cope, and afterwards, rerate your distress levels.

Rate your distress on the following scale:

1	2	3	4	5	6	7	8	9	10
No distress, calm				Moderate distress					Absolute panic

Date, time	What was the occasion?	Rating	What brought it on?	How did you try to cope?	Rerating
Monday 10.00	First day back at college. In the college lodge – David suggests I join him and some friends for lunch later on	8	Panic! I can't face students that I don't know. I won't be able to join in the conversation – they'll think I'm stupid. I am stupid!	Declined the offer	3
10.30	First lecture: sitting at the back, on my own – thinking about David	6	Misery. I am such a wimp – pathetic. I'll never get confident this way.	Left David a note to suggest lunch at my place tomorrow with just two of my friends	2
Friday 11.00pm	At Tony's party in the student common room. About 50 students	8	Anxiety. I don't know anyone, I dare not approach anyone and no one is going to approach me. I am failure.	Made my excuses to leave early and sat in my room brooding for two hours	3
Saturday 12.00	In town – saw a group of students from last night's party	8	Panic! They'll see me and recognize me as the wimp from the party. I am such a fool – I should have stayed.	Hid in the bookshop until they'd gone past. Went back to college quickly.	6

Diary 1(c): Obsessive–Compulsive Disorder

Monitor your stress levels each day, noting when you feel particularly worried, frightened or anxious. Use the diary as near to the time of distress as possible as it is easy to forget the details later. Record the occasion and rate the severity of your feelings (1–10). Where you can, note what triggered the stress – thoughts, images, feelings, events, for example. Also, record how you tried to cope, and afterwards, rerate your distress levels.

Rate your distress on the following scale:

1	2	3	4	5	6	7	8	9	10
No distress, calm				Moderate distress				Absolute panic	

Date, time	What was the occasion?	Rating	What brought it on?	How did you try to cope?	Rerating
Tues 3.00pm	Heard about car crash on the news. Whole family killed.	9	Picture in my mind of the pile up and my family being involved	Kept repeating my 'lucky' words and repeatedly phoned home to check that they were OK. No answer so kept telephoning for 2 hours	8
Thurs 10.00am	Reading the newspaper: story about cars catching fire because of faulty electrics	9	Saw myself in burning car and remembered that I should have had car serviced by now.	Shut the newspaper and didn't finish reading the story. Tried to forget. Repeated 'lucky' words over and over.	9
Sunday 3.30pm	Driving with Rosie when we went past a road traffic accident	9	Saw myself in the car crash. Thought 'it's your own fault because you've not had the car serviced'.	Talked through my fears which helped me see that they were exaggerated. Booked a car service!	3

The last question is particularly important as you must distinguish between the coping strategies which help and are good for you in the long run, and those which might make you feel better in the short term, but are not helpful over time.

To help you see how this sort of diary might be used, three examples are given in diaries 1(a)–(c). These are records made by a person with a dog phobia (1(a)); a person with social anxiety (1(b)); and someone with OCD (1(c)).

Getting to know your coping skills

When you review the last columns of your diary ('Rerating'), you will begin to see what strategies reduce your distress in the long and the short term and what responses to stress are not helpful at all. The strategies which are of no help can be dismissed straight away, leaving you to consider your 'short-term only' and 'long-term' coping methods.

'Short-term only' coping would include any response which gave immediate relief but which would be counter-productive if you kept on relying on it – for example, turning to tranquillizers or alcohol, avoiding difficult situations or scolding yourself. 'Short-term' strategies can be useful if they give you sufficient respite from distress for you then to put into action a 'long-term' strategy, or if the 'short-term' strategy is a planned last resort.

Consider the following example: a very tense business-man gets home from work far too stressed to settle. His relaxation exercise of choice is running and, if this is not possible, getting on with physical work around the house.

Generally, if he is unable to run or to busy himself, he would rely on talking through his stress with his wife; if she weren't available, he would telephone a friend. On this occasion, he gets ready to run but finds that he is too stressed and physically tense to engage in physical activity. Unfortunately, his wife is not at home and he cannot get his friend on the phone. He then falls back on his 'last resort' strategy and heads for the kitchen and starts to snack. Soon, he has unwound enough to go running after all.

Clearly, comfort eating would have been an unhelpful strategy if he had simply spent the evening overeating or if he routinely turned to eating in response to stress. However, in this instance, when his preferred strategies were not available to him, a snack enabled him to go on to a more healthy alternative.

It can be useful to make a list of your 'short-term only' strategies for reference when you are feeling stressed (see Figure 7.1).

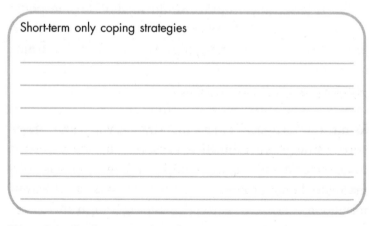

Figure 7.1 Coping strategies: short-term

'Long-term' coping strategies are those that are beneficial both in the short term and in the long term. However, their impact might not be as immediate as some of the 'short-term only' strategies, and therefore we often need more self-discipline to put them into action. In the example above, the businessman's 'long-term' strategies were physical activity and talking through his problems. Other 'long-term' coping skills could include yoga exercises, planning and problem-solving, or talking to yourself in a soothing constructive way. Again, it might be helpful for you to make a list of your long-term strategies (Figure 7.2).

Long-term only coping strategies

Figure 7.2   Coping strategies: long-term

Don't feel that you have to abandon all your 'short-term' coping strategies at once: this can be too alarming a prospect to be sensible. Instead, think how you might begin to integrate more helpful coping strategies into your repertoire of techniques.

A final note about coping with stress concerns the use

of stimulants. When you are trying to cope, it is especially important not to turn to substances such as alcohol and nicotine, or caffeine-containing food and drink such as chocolate, chocolate drinks, coffee, cola drinks or tea. In the short term these can provide a pleasant distraction from your problem; but as soon as the caffeine or nicotine enters your system, they will increase the unpleasant bodily symptoms and make managing your stress more difficult. Alcohol is deceptive, in that it *is* relaxing in the short term, however, the breakdown products (metabolites) of alcohol are stimulants, and so you can find yourself more tense than ever once the alcohol has been processed, or metabolized, by your body. Also, if you drink heavily, you can find yourself with a hangover which will impair your ability to cope. Instead, try to acquire a taste for decaffeinated or non-caffeinated drinks and foods, and try to cut back on smoking and drinking alcohol when you are stressed.

Using your diaries

When you have kept a diary of stress for a short while, you will become familiar with the way in which your problem presents itself and how you tend to deal with it. Study your diary and try to identify the vicious cycles which keep *your* problems going. Are your cycles of distress driven by bodily sensations, or by worrying thoughts, or by avoidance, or by a lack of social confidence, or by a lack of planning skills? If you need a reminder about the way in which problems are maintained, look back over Chapter 2 in Part One. When you have done this, you will be ready to read through

Table 7.1 Creating the best personal program

Coping strategy	When should I give this special attention?
Self-monitoring, diary-keeping	Throughout your program. This will help you to build up an accurate picture of your needs and will also provide a record of your progress.
Techniques for managing bodily sensations	
Controlled breathing	If you experience panic attacks, difficulty in breathing, dizziness. It is also a good idea to learn this as part of your relaxation training.
Applied relaxation	If you have much physical tension or bodily discomfort when you are stressed. This is also very helpful with sleep problems.
Techniques for managing psychological symptoms	
Distraction	If you have difficulty dismissing worries and upsetting mental images. This is also very useful in panic management.
Thought challenging	If distraction is not sufficient to manage your worrying thoughts. If you need a powerful and enduring means of self-reassurance.
Techniques for dealing with problem behaviors	
Graded exposure to fears	If you avoid what you fear, you *must* emphasize this, as exposure is the only sure way of overcoming a phobia or OCD.
Problem-solving strategies	If you have difficulty organizing your thoughts and making plans when you are under stress.
Assertiveness training	If interpersonal problems stress you.
Time management	If your stress management is undermined by poor organization/delegation.
Sleep management	If you are not getting enough sleep.
Techniques for coping in the long term	
Blueprinting	This is an essential part of the program for all users.
Coping with set-backs	This is essential and should be given attention throughout the program.

the following chapters in Part Two on self-help skills and
to relate the coping strategies to your problem(s).

From your diaries you should be able to see what bothers
you most when you are anxious and what keeps your problems going. Is it physical discomfort? If so, focus particularly
on the techniques for managing bodily sensations – especially if you find that you hyperventilate when stressed. If
worrying thoughts are your main source of stress, make
sure that you learn well the techniques of distraction and
thought challenging. Should you find that your main difficulty is rooted in avoidance and a lack of confidence, make
plans to prepare yourself for a program of graded exposure to your fears. If you discover that your fear is one of
interpersonal stress, emphasize the assertiveness training
in your personal program.

The coping strategies in this book are laid out so as to
make it easy for you to emphasize particular areas. The
summary in Table 7.1 will help you to decide which strategies will be most useful to you. It is advisable to try all
of the strategies, as you will most probably need to use
them in combination, but it is also important to remember
that each of us has different needs and different capacities,
so aim to tailor your self-help program to meet *your* needs
and reflect realistic goals for you.

SUMMARY

1 In order to manage your worries, fears and anxieties, you need to monitor them and become very familiar with their triggers and the sensations, thoughts and behavior which they evoke. You can do this through keeping a diary.

2 You also need to identify your current coping methods so that you can turn the useful ones to your best advantage, while limiting your use of the less helpful ones. Again, you can do this through diary keeping.

3 In order to manage your problems you will have to work through the entire self-help program.

4 You can use your records of *your* stress responses to identify your special needs. You should then match these with the different elements of the recovery program so that you can see which aspects of the program *you* should emphasize.

8

Managing bodily sensations: Controlled breathing

I was in agony, my chest hurt and my limbs ached. Now I realize that stress is very physical and I learnt how to keep the physical discomfort to a minimum simply by learning how to breathe properly. I had been breathing far too quickly and making matters worse for myself by doing so. Now, I take things easy, breathe slowly and am able to be more relaxed in stressful situations. I still get some discomfort but nothing that I can't tolerate.

Although breathing comes naturally and we can all do it, there is a comfortable and an uncomfortable way to breathe. The uncomfortable way is rapid and shallow breathing, which uses only the upper part of the lungs and results in the inhalation of too much oxygen. This is the sort of breathing that you will find yourself doing after you have just run to catch a bus or raced to get to an appointment on time. This rapid breathing is a perfectly normal response to exertion and stress and is called *hyperventilation*.

We all hyperventilate whenever we are tense or when

we are exercising. We breathe faster at these times in order to provide our muscles with oxygen to burn during activity. In this way, our body is prepared for action to relieve the stress – running away, for example – or to sustain the exercise. Rapid breathing is not troublesome in the short term – in fact, your body will need the extra oxygen if you have just run to catch a bus; but continued fast respiration causes physical discomfort which can be quite frightening.

Habitual overbreathing causes problems because it results in too much oxygen entering the bloodstream so that the usual oxygen-carbon dioxide balance is disturbed. As the oxygen level rises the relative carbon dioxide level falls, and this imbalance causes many unpleasant physical symptoms, which could include:

- tingling face, hands or limbs;
- muscle tremors and cramps;
- dizziness and visual problems;
- difficulty in breathing;
- exhaustion and feelings of fatigue;
- chest and stomach pains.

Understandably, these sensations can be very alarming, and so they often trigger more anxiety and therefore more hyperventilation. This can then set up another cycle of stress and can often lead to a panic attack. Figure 8.1 shows how this cycle of reactions can escalate.

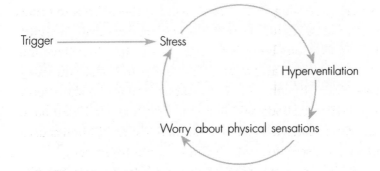

Figure 8.1 Hyperventilation and stress

Although it is common to worry about losing control, this is very unlikely. You can easily learn to correct overbreathing and control the symptoms for yourself by simply developing the habit of correct breathing. This means learning to breathe gently and evenly, through your nose, filling your lungs completely and then exhaling slowly and fully. The breathing exercise outlined below will help you to develop the ability to control the symptoms of hyperventilation.

The breathing exercise

Use your lungs fully and avoid breathing from your upper chest alone. Breathing should be a smooth action, without any gulping or gasping. When you first practise, it can be easier to do this exercise lying down, so that you can better feel the difference between shallow and deep breathing. As you become more practised, you can try the exercise sitting or standing.

- Place one hand on your chest and one on your stomach.
- As you breathe in through your nose, allow your stomach to swell. This means that you are using your lungs fully. Try to keep the movement in your upper chest to a minimum and keep the movement gentle.
- Slowly and evenly, breathe out through your nose.
- Repeat this, trying to get a rhythm going. You are aiming to take eight to twelve breaths a minute: breathing in and breathing out again counts as one breath. This might be difficult to gauge at first, so practise counting five to seven seconds for a complete breathing cycle (i.e. breathing in and out).
- *Do not deep breathe rapidly.*

Controlled breathing in action: Managing a panic attack

After my very first panic attack, I was really sensitive to every bodily sensation – especially discomfort in my chest. When I had the first attack, I was sure that the ache in my chest meant that I was having a heart attack. That fear stayed with me even though my doctor had helped me to recognize that I had a healthy heart and that we all suffer aches and pains from time to time. His words reassured me in the surgery, but as soon as I had the chest pains again, I began to panic.

Then he tried something else. He explained how we all breathe quickly when we are frightened and this can bring on chest pains, which in my case made me more frightened, and so I breathed even faster, and so on. I wasn't convinced at first, but after he had shown me how to breathe slowly and evenly, he asked me to start panting in the surgery. Well, it was a real lesson to me. Within seconds of beginning to pant, I started to get the chest pain and the dizziness just like when I have the 'heart attacks'. Next, he began to talk me through controlled breathing, and my dizziness went away and the chest pains eased. He asked me to do the exercise again, and again I seemed to be able to switch on and switch off the symptoms.

After that, I was more confident and I found that, whenever I got anxious, the controlled breathing would take the edge off my fear. The doctor told me to practise slow breathing during the day so that it would become a habit. So, every time I go to the bathroom, where it's nice and peaceful, I spend two or three minutes doing my breathing exercises. I find it really relaxing and I get to practise half a dozen times a day. As time goes on, I am getting better and better at switching off the sensations and they bother me less and less.

Difficulties when using controlled breathing

Difficulty in breathing naturally

At first you may feel that you are not getting enough air, but with practice you will find this slower rate of breathing is comfortable. If you continue to feel that you can't breathe in deeply, begin the exercise by exhaling as much as you can. In this way, you will empty your lungs and the in-breath should be deep and comfortable.

Forgetting to practise

It is important to practise the exercise whenever you can, as you are trying to develop a new habit which will only come through repeated rehearsal. To help you to practise, try putting a coloured spot somewhere eye-catching to remind you to use correct breathing each time you see it. A small dot of bright nail varnish should do the trick; or try a sticky spot from a memo board. You might find it useful to put the marker on your watch, as most of us look at our watches very regularly throughout the day.

As your skill improves, you will find it easier and easier to switch to correct breathing whenever you feel anxious. As with all anxiety management techniques, you will be most successful if you tackle your stress when it is at a low level.

SUMMARY

1 Everyone breathes more rapidly when under stress. When hyperventilation goes on too long or happens in the absence of stress, very unpleasant physical sensations result.

2 These sensations can be controlled by breathing slowly and smoothly through the nose and filling the lungs completely.

3 In order for this to be effective the technique of controlled breathing must be very well rehearsed.

9

Managing bodily sensations: Applied relaxation

My tense and panicky feelings began to diminish as soon as I began to do my relaxation exercises regularly. At first, I hadn't done them often enough and I did not get much benefit. Then I decided to make a real effort and it paid off. I found that I got mental relief as well as physical relaxation and this gave me hope that I could learn to manage my anxiety. Now I can feel relaxed very quickly and I can 'switch off' the tension in all sorts of situations which used to bother me.

Under stress, the muscles in our bodies tense, and muscular tension causes uncomfortable sensations such as headache, stiff neck, painful shoulders, tight chest, difficulty in breathing, trembling, churning stomach, difficulty in swallowing, blurred vision and back pain. Of course, these sensations can trigger more tension and so a vicious cycle is set up.

The most effective way of controlling bodily tension is learning how to relax in response to tension. This applied relaxation isn't just a matter of sitting in front of the television or having a hobby (although these recreations are important

too); applied relaxation means developing a skill which
enables you to reduce physical tension whenever you need
to. You can then relieve anxiety and the associated
unpleasant bodily sensations in a variety of situations.
Furthermore, when your body is free of tension, your mind
tends to be relaxed, too.

The ability to relax at will is achieved by progressing
through a series of structured exercises, such as the four
which follow. These are designed to help you learn to relax
step-by-step. The first two routines are quite long and you
may find that taped instructions are helpful. You can make
your own tape following the relaxation script (*see*
pp. 207–18), being sure to use slow, gentle speech.

General guidelines for relaxing

- Plan when you will practise, and try to keep to this
  time each day so that you develop a routine that
  you will be able to stick to.
- Practise the relaxation routine two or three times a
  day: the more you practise the more easily you will
  be able to relax.
- Make sure that you choose somewhere quiet to practise, and that no one will disturb you during your
  relaxation exercises.
- Do not attempt your exercise if you are hungry or
  have just eaten; or if the room is too hot or too chilly.
  This will make it difficult to relax.

- Start the exercise by lying down in a comfortable position, wearing comfortable clothes. Later, you can also practise relaxation while you are sitting or standing.
- Try to adopt a 'passive attitude', which means not worrying about your performance or whether you are successfully relaxing. Just 'have a go' and let it happen.
- *Breathing* is important: try to breathe through your nose, filling your lungs completely so that you feel your stomach muscles stretch. Breathe slowly and regularly. It is important that you do not take a lot of quick, deep breaths as this can make you feel dizzy or faint and even make your tension worse. If you place your hands on your stomach, you will feel movement if you are breathing properly. Try this out before you exercise to make sure that you are used to the feeling.
- Record your progress so that you can assess if the relaxation procedure is working for you. Use a record sheet like the one overleaf to keep details of your experiences. Expect day-to-day variation in your ability to relax – we all have days when relaxation comes easily and other days when it is more difficult.

Diary 2 Logging relaxation techniques

Record your level of relaxation before and after each exercise (1–10). Note any relevant information, such as the sort of day you are having, where you are, things on your mind. Use your record to discover where and when you are best able to relax and to monitor your progress.

Rate your distress on the following scale:

1	2	3	4	5	6	7	8	9	10
Not relaxed, tense				Moderate relaxation					Very relaxed, no tension

Date, time	Rating before	Which exercise did you use?	Rating afterwards	Notes

The exercises

As you will not be able to relax and read the instructions at the same time, first familiarize yourself with all the exercises. You can then start to work through the routines, which get progressively shorter. When you are able to relax using the first exercise, move on to exercise two; when you have mastered this, begin exercise three. Finally, learn exercise four, which is a rapid relaxation routine. This whole process should be done gradually, over several weeks. The length of time needed will vary from person to person, so don't worry that you are not progressing fast enough as this will diminish your ability to relax. Only move to the next exercise when you feel fully relaxed at the end of a routine: there is nothing to be gained by rushing through the program.

Progressive muscular relaxation (PMR)

PMR is a well-established relaxation routine which was devised by Edmund Jacobsen in the 1930s. His aim was to develop a systematic programme which would achieve a deep level of relaxation. His solution was a series of tense–relax exercises focusing on the body's major muscle groups. An additional advantage of this approach is that you will also learn to make the distinction between tense and relaxed muscles, so that you can better recognize when you are tense and then relax in response to this.

The basic movement which you use at every stage of the exercise is as follows:

Tense your muscles, but do not strain, and concentrate on the sensation of tension. Hold this for about five seconds and then let go of the tension for ten to fifteen seconds. Discover how your muscles feel when you relax them.

PMR requires you to do this for muscle groups throughout the body. It is important to breathe slowly and regularly between each stage in the procedure and during the exercise. In your chosen place and position, focus in turn on parts of the body, as follows:

- *Feet*   Pull your toes back, tense the muscles in your feet. Relax and repeat.
- *Legs*   Straighten your legs, point your toes towards your face. Relax, let your legs go limp and repeat.
- *Abdomen*   Tense your stomach muscles by pulling them in and up – as if preparing to receive a punch. Relax and repeat.
- *Back*   Arch your back. Relax and repeat.
- *Shoulders/neck*   Shrug your shoulders as hard as you can, bringing them up and in. Press your head back. Relax and repeat.
- *Arms*   Stretch out your arms and hands. Relax, let your arms hang limp and repeat.
- *Face*   Tense your forehead and jaw. Lower your eyebrows and bite hard. Relax and repeat.
- *Whole body*   Tense your entire body: feet, legs, abdomen, back, shoulders and neck, arms, and face. Hold the tension for a few seconds. Relax and repeat.

If you still feel tense when you reach the end of the routine, go through it again. If only parts of your body feel tense, repeat the exercise in those areas. When you have finished the exercise and feel relaxed, spend a few moments relaxing your mind. Think about something restful: whatever scene or image works best for you. Breathe slowly through your nose, filling your lungs completely. Continue for a minute or two, then open your eyes. Do not stand up straight away; when you are ready, move *slowly* and stretch *gently*.

PMR should be practised about twice a day until you always feel fully relaxed at the end of the exercise. Then you can move on to shortened PMR. Remember, it takes time to learn how to relax. Give yourself a chance and do not expect to succeed too soon. Some people find it easier to follow this exercise if they have taped instructions to guide them. As mentioned earlier you can make your own audio-tape by reading the relaxation script. Be sure to speak slowly and gently.

PMR in action: Managing sleep problems

After my operation, I was quite ill and it took me some time to get back to being my old self. However, I never did get rid of the general aches and pains which I developed during my recuperation. My worry was that I had not completely recovered and that I was going to relapse and become ill again. My doctor was very helpful and she organized a range of tests so that she could rule out illness. All the tests were negative and I must say that I was relieved when she showed them to me.

Unfortunately, the aches did not go away and they were particularly troublesome at night.

I've never been a 'good' sleeper and it usually takes me a while to drift off, but I became a terrible sleeper after my illness and one of the thoughts that used to keep me awake was: 'I'll never be able to get to sleep while I'm this uncomfortable' and pretty soon I would also begin thinking: 'Perhaps I am getting ill again!' These thoughts and the physical discomfort would keep me awake for hours. Needless to say, the next day I would feel tired and the aches and pains would seem worse.

My doctor explained that the aches and worries were probably feeding on each other and contributing to my sleeplessness. She went on to say that I could break out of this vicious cycle if I learnt to relax when I was trying to go to sleep. She described a relaxation exercise which involved systematically untensing all the muscle groups in my body and she gave me a tape of instructions to follow at home. I then practised relaxing with the tape once or twice daily. This was no hardship because it gave me relief from my aches and pains during the day.

I soon knew the exercise well enough to be able to use it when I went to bed. Instead of dwelling on the discomfort in my body, I focused on relaxing my body and I rarely stayed awake long enough to complete the exercise! I would then wake up better able to cope with the strains of the next day, and if I did get very achey, I would simply do the relaxation exercise in a chair. It's made a real difference to me.

Shortened PMR

You can begin to shorten the routine of relaxing by missing out the 'tense' stage. Simply go through the sequence of systematically relaxing the different muscle groups. When you can do this effectively, you can adapt the routine to use at other times and in other places. For example, you might try the exercise sitting, rather than lying down; or you might move from a quiet bedroom to the living area which is not so peaceful. In this way, you will be learning to relax in a range of environments, which is what you need for real-life coping.

Simple relaxation routine

This is an even shorter exercise which you can practise as you become more experienced at achieving the relaxed state. It was developed in the 1970s by a cardiologist named Herbert Benson who wanted to help cardiac patients reduce the stress that worsened their physical condition. However, it has become established as a universally helpful relaxation technique. For the exercise, you will need to find a restful mental device to use during the routine. You might use a sound or word which you find relaxing, such as the word 'calm' or the sound of the sea; or a particular object which is restful, perhaps a picture or an ornament that you like; or a scene you find calming, such as a quiet country spot or a deserted beach.

When you have worked out what is most effective for you follow these instructions:

- Sit in a comfortable position with your eyes closed. Imagine your body growing heavier and more relaxed.
- Breathe through your nose and become aware of your breathing as you inhale. As you breathe out, think about your mental image, while breathing easily and naturally.
- Don't worry whether or not you are good at the exercise; simply let go of your tensions and relax at your own pace. Distracting thoughts will probably come into your mind. Don't worry about this and don't dwell on them; simply return to thinking of your mental image or your breathing pattern.
- You can keep this going for as long as it takes you to feel relaxed. This might be two minutes or twenty minutes: the criterion for finishing the exercise is your feeling of relaxation. When you do finish, sit quietly with your eyes closed for a few moments, and then sit with your eyes open. Don't stand up or begin moving around too quickly.

As this is a brief exercise, you can practise it more frequently than the earlier ones. You could practise for a few minutes every hour; or at coffee, lunch and tea breaks; or between appointments; or at every service station if you are driving on a long journey and feeling stressed. The options are endless and the most useful thing you can do is to discover what fits in best with your lifestyle.

Simple relaxation in action: Managing health worries

My family has always said that my problem is that I never unwind and that's why I feel so tense and physically unwell all the time. The truth was that I didn't know how to unwind. I'd tried sitting with a book or watching TV, but my mind always wandered back to some worry or other and I'd soon become tense and uncomfortable again. Then I learnt a simple relaxation routine which gave me something constructive to focus on as well as easing the aches and pains that used to concern me so much.

I had to find a few minutes each day, at regular intervals, to sit and concentrate on breathing calmly and then imagining a soothing scene. My first choice didn't work too well – it was a tropical beach and I thought of myself lying in the sun, listening to the sea. I'm such an active person that this quickly began to irritate me! My next choice did work. I remembered a formal garden that we had visited earlier in the year and which I'd loved. So, in my mind, I went for a stroll around this garden, noticing all the different trees, shrubs and flowers and imagining the scent of the roses and the feel of the sun on my shoulders. I managed to find a postcard of the garden which helped make my mental picture more vivid.

I did this exercise three or four times a day – whenever I got to the end of one chore and before I began the next. It was wonderful. No physical pains to worry me and I found that I had more energy if I relaxed during the day. Every now and then I get a twinge or an ache and I am alarmed, but I use this as my cue to relax and, so far, the discomfort has always gone away.

Cued relaxation

When you are able to relax using these three exercises, you can begin to use your relaxation skills throughout the day and not just at your designated 'relaxation time'. In this way, you will progress towards being able to relax at will. All you need for cued relaxation is something which will catch your eye regularly and remind you to:

- drop your shoulders;
- untense the muscles in your body;
- check your breathing;
- relax.

As a cue, or reminder, you could use a small, coloured spot on your watch or something else which you look at regularly during the day. Every time you see the cue, you will be reminded to relax and so you will be practising your relaxation skills several times a day. There are all sorts of cues which you might use; work out what catches your eye frequently and use this as a reminder.

Applied relaxation

The final stage of relaxation training is its application whenever you need to use it. With time and regular practice, relaxation will become a way of life and you will be able to relax at will. Of course, you are bound to continue to experience some tension from time to time – this is normal – but you will now have a better awareness of it and the skills to bring it under control.

A useful analogy for relaxation training is learning to play the piano. You would start with the laborious, but necessary, scales (PMR) and graduate to arpeggios (shortened PMR). With this as a foundation, you would be able to play simple tunes (simple relaxation) and gradually more sophisticated music (cued relaxation). Only after a lot of practice would you be able to sit at a piano and play spontaneously (applied relaxation). You would fail at spontaneous piano playing if you had not worked through the earlier stages, and you can fail to relax if you have not done the groundwork.

Applied relaxation in action: Managing GAD

It was helpful for the psychologist to give me a label for my problem – GAD – but I was still plagued with the worrying and the tension. She explained that it would take time to get the GAD under control and that she would first teach me how to relax my body and mind. I remember thinking that I had tried everything to relax and that she wasn't going to teach me anything new. I told her that I'd hired romantic videos, I'd gone out to dinner with friends, I'd even joined an exercise class. Then she explained that she was going to teach me a further way to relax so that I could add this to my list of relaxing activities.

Her method was different from my other relaxing activities because I did the exercise alone and focused on myself and the way I felt. It was quite difficult to get into at first, especially as the early exercises took fifteen to twenty minutes and they were a bit boring. As the exercises got shorter, I began to enjoy them more and I was more motivated to practise. However, I didn't think that it was going to take so long – I spent weeks learning to relax!

Eventually, I reached the stage of being able to identify when I was tense and then I was able to drop my shoulders, regulate my breathing and empty my mind of worries. This is no mean feat, believe me. It was hard work and I nearly gave up several times, but now I'm glad I persevered because it has changed the way I feel. I am no longer dogged by that sense of doom and gloom because I can shake it off by relaxing whenever and wherever I need to.

Difficulties in relaxing

Relaxation training is not without problems. Some of the most common are the following.

Peculiar feelings when doing the exercises

It is usual to feel strange if you are doing something physical that you are not used to. Don't worry about this, as your tension will rise if you do. Try to accept that it will take a few practice sessions before you begin to feel comfortable with the exercises and you will find that the unusual sensations will soon disappear. Also, make sure that you are not hyperventilating during the exercise, or standing up and moving around too soon, or practising when you are too hungry or full, as this can cause unpleasant feelings when you try to relax.

Cramp

This can be painful but never dangerous. Avoid tensing your muscles too vigorously and use a warm room for your practice. Ease the pain by rubbing the affected muscle; then you can resume your exercise – gently.

Falling asleep

Sometimes this is what you will hope for, but if sleep isn't the object of your exercise, you can try not lying down as this tends to encourage sleeping. You could also hold something (unbreakable) so that you would drop it and wake if you dozed off.

Intruding and worrying thoughts

These are quite normal and not a serious obstacle to your practice. The best way of making sure that the thoughts go away is by not dwelling on them. Try to accept that they will drift into your mind from time to time and then simply refocus on your relaxation exercise. If you try *not* to think of the intrusive thoughts, they will not go away.

Not feeling relaxed

This can be a problem when you first begin relaxation training. When you are new to the exercise, you may not feel much benefit, because the benefits come with practice. The most important thing is not to try too hard as this will create tension. Just let the sensations of relaxation happen when they happen. It is also worth asking yourself whether you have made your environment conducive to relaxation.

SUMMARY

1 Stress causes muscular tension, which gives rise to a range of unpleasant physical sensations.

2 These unpleasant feelings can be controlled by learning and practising a series of relaxation exercises: this takes time.

3 Eventually one can respond to physical tension by using relaxation to offset the physical discomfort.

4 Physical relaxation has the benefit of promoting mental tranquillity.

10

Managing psychological symptoms: Distraction

What I liked about distraction was its simplicity. Instead of dwelling on my worries and feeling worse and worse, I learnt to switch off from them. With practice, I became more efficient and I found that I could do this in almost any situation. Furthermore, I discovered that nothing terrible happened if I didn't worry and that I'd been wasting such a lot of time, in the past, fretting about things.

In this chapter and the next we will focus on strategies for keeping psychological aspects of worry, fear and anxiety under control. This means addressing the worrying thoughts and images that are associated with distress. Sometimes these are easily identified; sometimes you might simply be aware of feeling fear or anxiety and it will have seemed to come out of the blue.

What triggers psychological symptoms?

Sometimes it is difficult to articulate what is going through your mind because the link is so well established that the reaction seems to happen automatically. This can apply to pleasant or to stressful reactions. A pleasant automatic response might occur as you walked by a bonfire or smelt old paint and felt contented without realizing why. If you thought about it you might discover that this was because the smells reminded you of happy childhood experiences of firework displays or helping your grandpa in the shed. Even when the automatic response is a stress reaction, it is often no bad thing: when a car comes round the corner too quickly, you jump out of the way; if a child looks as though he is about to stumble into a fire, you grab him. There is a chain of reasoning behind such actions; but it becomes so well established that it is almost as if we short-circuit the conscious thinking process and thus save precious time in dangerous situations.

This 'short-circuiting' can underpin problem anxiety, too. Imagine a woman who is happily walking round a church filled with flowers. She suddenly has a surge of anxiety and feels compelled to flee from the church, which spoils her enjoyment. Later, she realizes that her feelings of distress were triggered because she smelled chrysanthemums, which took her back to childhood when she was terrified of her piano teacher who always had a pot of them on the piano. On this occasion she 'short-circuited' the reasoning process and suffered inappropriate feelings of distress.

As we have already noted, cycles of worrying thoughts and increasing anxiety can develop which will keep tensions high. For example, at a party, symptoms of anxiety such as blushing or not being able to speak easily would cause more worry and increase stress and social worries. A cycle of social anxiety could develop. If the situation were one where someone had a slight chest pain and thought: 'This could be a heart attack!', stress levels would rise and the person would experience symptoms such as increased muscular tension, which would worsen the pain, and so the thoughts might become even more alarming: 'This *is* a heart attack!' The anxiety would get worse and a cycle of increasing tension would develop.

Whether or not you can put your finger on the mental component, alarming thoughts or images keep anxiety going and the symptoms of anxiety maintain the alarming thoughts. There are, however, two ways of breaking the cycles of worrying thoughts: *distraction*, which refocuses attention away from the cycle, and *challenging*, which helps rationalize exaggerated worries. Distraction is dealt with here; challenging is covered in the next chapter.

Distraction

It is possible to concentrate on only one thing at once, so when you turn your attention to something which is neutral or pleasant, you can distract yourself from worrying thoughts and images. By using specific techniques of distraction, you can break the cycle of worrying thoughts and prevent your anxiety increasing.

There are three basic distraction techniques which you can tailor to suit your needs. These are: *physical exercise; refocusing*; and *mental exercise*. The key to successful distraction lies in finding something which needs a great deal of attention, is very specific, and holds some interest for you.

If a distraction task is too simple, too vague or too boring, it tends not to be effective.

Physical exercise

This simply means keeping active when you are stressed. If you are physically occupied, you are less likely to be able to dwell on worrying thoughts. You could try taking exercise such as walking, jogging, playing squash and so on. These sorts of activities are particularly beneficial as they help use up the adrenaline which can otherwise make you feel tense. If, at a party, you began to feel self-conscious, you might offer to take drinks around to people to keep yourself and your mind busy. If your physical task requires mental effort, so much the better, because the distraction effect will be more powerful.

In different situations you will need different activities. You might play squash in the evening in order to work off the day's stress; take a brief walk up and down the corridor when you are very tense at the office; reorganize your desk when you are not able to leave the office but are alone; unwind and rewind paper clips to take the edge off your anxiety in meetings. Other distractions that you might try are taking the dog for a walk, reorganizing your garage or a room in the house if you are unable to go out, tidying your handbag, updating your diary if you are physically restricted in what you can do – in a doctor's waiting room, for example.

Refocusing

This means distracting yourself by paying great attention to things around you. If you were in a crowded street you could try counting the number of men and women you could see with blonde hair, or look for certain objects in a shop window; in a café, you could listen to others' conversations or study the details of someone's dress or of a picture. You don't have to be sophisticated, you just need to find a range of objects to absorb your attention. For example, if a woman were anxious about using the supermarket, she could read car number plates as her friend drove her to the store, attend closely to her shopping list while moving round the supermarket and, at the checkout, read the details on food packages, count the number of items in her own or another person's basket or browse through a magazine.

Mental exercise

This requires you to be more creative and to use more mental effort by generating a distracting phrase, picture or mental exercise for yourself. You might try reciting some poetry, recalling a favourite holiday trip, practising mental arithmetic or studying someone nearby and trying to guess what they do, what interests they might have, where they are going and so on. You could try dwelling on an imaginary scene to take your mind away from worrying thoughts; by making your scene come alive with colour and sounds and texture, you can distract yourself even better. Examples of this would be imagining your dream home and then walking through every room, studying detail; 'listening' to a well-loved tune; cycling over a familiar and much-loved track, paying attention to the scenery; recalling all the stages involved in making a complex flower display; or redesigning your home. The more detailed the mental tasks, the more distracting they are.

General rules for distraction

- Before you use a distraction technique you must select one which is suited to you and the situation in which you need to be distracted. There is no point in dwelling on a picture of a sunsoaked beach if you hate the sea and you sunburn easily, or if your real love is skiing. Similarly, relying on physical activity to distract you will not be helpful if your anxiety attacks happen during interviews. Work out your preferences and needs and then tailor distraction to suit you. Try to make use of your own interests: if you are a keen gardener, you might use pruning and weeding as your physical activity; looking through the bus window at gardens and identifying plants as a refocusing exercise; and holding an image of a beautiful formal garden as a mental task.

- When you have established what you need, be inventive in developing your own selection of distraction techniques, but always be specific in your choice of task and choose exercises that demand a lot of attention.

- When you have a repertoire of distraction techniques for different occasions, practise them whenever you have the chance. In this way, when you are stressed, you can switch your thoughts to your distraction quite easily.

Now consider when and where you could use distraction techniques by recalling the situations you find difficult and then planning which of your techniques you might use. An example is shown in Figure 10.1. Try compiling a list for yourself using the blank Figure 10.2, or on a separate piece of paper.

My anxiety-provoking situation(s)	My distraction technique
Sitting in stationary traffic	Listen to soothing music
Waiting in doctor's clinic	Read book/magazine

Figure 10.1   Sample of distraction technique

Give your distraction techniques a try. Use them when you are feeling anxious and see what happens. If the technique isn't very effective, think why this might be and try to do something about it.

My anxiety-provoking situation(s)	My distraction technique
_____	_____
_____	_____
_____	_____
_____	_____
_____	_____
_____	_____
_____	_____
_____	_____
_____	_____

Figure 10.2 List of distraction techniques for anxiety-provoking situations

Distraction in action: Managing claustrophobia

I just can't bear enclosed spaces – I'm all right in the street where I can breathe and I can manage at home because I feel relaxed there. But theatres, churches, lifts, crowded shops: no! I had accepted that I wouldn't be able to get about as much as most people, but it wasn't too much of a burden: we hired videos, I went shopping in the week when things are quite quiet and I never felt inclined to go to church, anyhow. However, things changed. It seemed that my children and my nieces and nephews were all getting married and having babies and then having them baptized. Suddenly, I was expected to go to church and go into hospitals. I was so torn. I wanted to see my children married and my grandchildren baptized but I was also terrified and I wanted to stay away.

Fortunately, I discovered a way of getting through the ceremonies – although I always sat near the back of the church so that I could escape, if necessary. I taught myself ways of distracting my mind from my panicky thoughts. There were three things which helped me. First, I always carried a really good book so that I could get lost in that if we had to sit around for any length of time. I know that it might seem rude to sit in a pew reading until the bride arrives, but it was often that or not going to the wedding. Second, I took my worry beads with me everywhere I went so that I could fiddle with them to take my mind off my worries – these were more acceptable in church but alarmed a few visitors at the hospital! Finally, I taught myself a sort of meditation: I would be able to stand or sit, just like everyone else, but I imagined that I was somewhere else, somewhere safe. In my imagination I was back on the farm where I grew up and I could imagine walking through our fields with my father.

These strategies have enabled me to be present at some of the most important occasions of my life and, little by little, I feel more confident about attending the next one.

Difficulties in using distraction

If your strategy does not work well, this could be because:

- You are not practised enough. You need to practise more, especially when you are not anxious.
- The technique was not suited to the situation. Think what other strategies you have in your repertoire and give them a try.
- You were already too stressed to manage your anxiety effectively. Try to catch your anxiety earlier next time – any coping technique will work better if you are less stressed.

A final note: Many people find distraction invaluable in dealing with worries, fears and anxieties, and it can give you an opportunity to think and plan more productively. However, it does not suit everyone and it can even be counterproductive if it is used as a means of avoiding difficult situations. For example, if you were anxious about speaking with guests at social gatherings and you always distracted yourself by handing round the drinks, then you would never face your real fear and it would not go away. If this applies to you, you need to try a different means of thought management, namely 'challenging'; this is described in the next chapter.

SUMMARY

1 Worrying thoughts and images can trigger a cycle of increasing anxiety.

2 It is possible to distract yourself from the worries, and so break this cycle, by using techniques of physical exercise; refocusing; and mental exercise.

3 These techniques have to be personalized and practised to be effective.

11

Managing psychological symptoms: Challenging worrying thoughts and images

I had always known just what thoughts set off my worrying and feeling miserable, but it had never occurred to me to ask myself if these thoughts were reasonable. When I started to do so, I found that I could challenge most of my worrying thoughts and that took the sting out of them. Sometimes, I enlisted my partner's help in questioning a negative thought and between us we've managed to make life a lot more bearable for both of us.

The technique of challenging requires you to recognize a worrying thought and ask yourself. 'Is this a realistic worry?' If it isn't a realistic concern, you need to replace it with a constructive statement. You already know that anxiety causes us to think differently and that we can get caught up in a cycle of worry and increasing anxiety. Challenging is another way of interrupting the cycle of increasing tension by decreasing the impact of the worrying thoughts.

It is not always easy to recognize unrealistic worries and to rationalize them, but the procedure described in this

Diary 3 Thought diary

Monitor your stress levels each day, noting when you feel particularly worried, frightened or anxious. Use the diary as near to the time of distress as possible as it is easy to forget the details later. Rate the severity of your feelings (1–10). and note what thoughts or images triggered the distress. Then look for thinking biases and try to challenge your stress-provoking thoughts. Afterwards, rerate your distress level.

Rate your distress on the following scale:

1	2	3	4	5	6	7	8	9	10

No distress, calm   Moderate distress   Absolute panic

Date, time	What was going through your mind?	Rating	Thinking biases	How can you challenge this?	Rerating

Accurately describing your fear

chapter should help you to develop the skill of checking out your automatic thoughts and images. First, however, you must be able to identify anxious thoughts. Your best cue is feeling anxious. When you are aware of your tension rising, ask yourself: 'What is going through my mind?' Your worries may be in the form of sentences, such as 'I am going to make a fool of myself', or 'I think that I am having a heart attack', or in the form of a picture, such as a scene where you are losing control or an image of something terrible happening. It is not always easy to recognize worrying thoughts and images, but with practice you will become better able to identify what is going through your mind.

A very helpful and structured procedure for challenging stressful thoughts and images was developed by an American psychiatrist, Dr Aaron T. Beck, in the 1970s and 1980s. The strategy he suggests involves three steps: identifying what is going through your mind; questioning this; and finding a rational alternative.

Identification of worrying thoughts and images

When you are feeling calm, it is not always easy to recall the thoughts or images that triggered your anxiety. Keeping a record of what goes through your mind near the time of the anxious episode can be the best way of discovering the words, images or phrases that cause your tension. Use the thought diary (Diary 3, page 120 and at end of book) as a daily record, writing down whatever is in your mind when you are anxious.

With practice, this task will become easier; but if you do continue to find this exercise difficult, remember that timing is important: if you do not 'catch' a thought as it occurs, you can lose it. Also, try not to shy away from examining what you feel and think. Although in the short term you may feel upset by looking closely at your thoughts, in doing so you will eventually be able to take control of your worries and anxiety.

Questioning anxious thoughts

When you have recorded your stressful thoughts, you will need to look for the common thinking biases which, you will remember, fall into the general categories of:

- *catastrophizing*: anticipating total disaster if something minor goes wrong;
- *black-and-white thinking*: viewing things in 'all or nothing' terms and overlooking degree and compromise;
- *exaggerating*: magnifying negative or weak aspects, forgetting the positive aspects and the signs of your strengths;
- *overgeneralizing*: concluding *everything* to be awful *always* because of one bad experience;
- *ignoring the positive*: overlooking personal strengths and good experiences and dwelling on the negative aspects of yourself and your life;
- *scanning*: searching for the thing you fear.

At this stage you are trying to evaluate whether or not your thoughts are rational. At the time of feeling anxious or worried, you might not be able to spot irrational thinking patterns or predictions; if that is the case, look at your record later, when you are feeling calm and more able to view the situation clearly. If you still have difficulty in gaining a rational perspective, ask a friend to look through your diary entries and to comment on the accuracy of your perceptions and predictions.

Finding alternative ways of thinking

When you are familiar with the mental component of your anxiety and the particular thinking biases to which you are prone, you can begin to find constructive alternatives to anxiety-promoting thinking. Rational thinking will make you feel less anxious and better able to cope with difficulties.

There are five questions you should ask yourself in order to generate a more confident way of thinking:

- *Are there reasons for my having this worrying thought?* This will help you to understand why you have the worry and make it less likely that you feel silly or embarrassed about it.
- *Are there reasons against my holding this thought?* Now you are beginning to look for evidence to undermine and weaken your worry. You might use a friend or a partner to help you find statements to challenge your worry.

- *What is the worst thing that could happen?* Be brave and consider the worst outcome of the situation that bothers you.
- *How could I cope with this?* Now work out a plan for coping in the worst situation. If you can cope with the worst thing that could happen, you can feel confident that you can manage your anxiety. Reflect on your own assets and skills and on your successful coping experiences in the past. Think about how you might change the problem situation or change how you feel about it. Also consider how others can help: what advice and support are available from family, friends or professionals? Again, you might find it helpful to get someone else's views on this.
- *What is a more constructive way of viewing the situation?* Look back over the notes you have made and try to form a new, rational statement in response to your initial worry.

Challenging is a demanding technique, and when you first start to do this exercise you might find that it takes you some time and that you need to keep notes. A few examples might help you to see how this strategy can be used.

Challenging in Action, 1: Anxieties about a Friend

'Sara is late for our meeting. She might have had a car crash and have been injured.'

1 *Are there reasons for my having this worrying thought?* Yes, there are: I read about people being killed in road accidents and she is travelling on a main road where she could have an accident. So I am not being completely ridiculous.

2 *Are there reasons against my holding this thought?* Yes, there are: plenty of people use that road day in and day out and never have an accident. The weather conditions today are very good for driving and so an accident is even less likely than usual. Even if Sara were in an accident, she need not be badly hurt – quite a few of my friends have had accidents and experienced very minor injuries, if any. There are road works on the road she uses – they could account for her being late.

3 *What is the worst thing that could happen?* The worst thing is that she's had an accident and is injured.

4 *How would I cope with this?* This would be a difficult situation for me, but I could get my husband to support me. We could contact the accident services at the hospital to find out how badly she'd been hurt. I would want to visit and could take my husband with me. I would tell myself that she will be well looked after in the hospital.

5 *What is a more constructive way of viewing the situation?* It is unlikely that Sara has had an accident and she's probably late because of road works. If she has had an accident, then she is not necessarily badly injured; and if she were, I could reassure myself that the hospital staff are the best people to deal with this and use my husband to support me if I am distressed.

Challenging in Action, 2: Dealing with Physical Symptoms

'I feel dizzy and light-headed. I am beginning to sweat and feel sick. I am sure that I am going to pass out in this shop and make a fool of myself.'

1 *Are there reasons for my having this worrying thought?* Yes, there are: my friend works in a shop and says that customers frequently feel faint and sometimes pass out in public. I once fainted in church, so I know that it is possible.

2 *Are there reasons against my holding this thought?* Yes, there are: I often feel like this when I am anxious. I now know that I am experiencing symptoms of anxiety – and I know that worrying and overbreathing will make them worse.

3 *What is the worst thing that could happen?* The worst thing is that I would faint here in the shop and I would look foolish.

4 *How would I cope with this?* I could find a chair and ask someone to help me. Meanwhile, I can practise my controlled breathing and brief relaxation exercises. If I did actually faint, someone would come to my rescue: my friend says that shop staff are always ready to deal with this kind of emergency.

5 *What is a more constructive way of viewing the situation?* It is very hot in here and that could have triggered these unpleasant feelings; my anxiety is probably making them worse and I know that I can control things by finding a quiet spot and using my anxiety management skills. Even if I fainted, I would recover and feel all right, as I did after I'd passed out in church. However, I was ill at that time and I am not ill now. My friend says that people do feel faint in large shops, so a staff member won't be surprised if I ask for help. I never think that someone is foolish if they feel unwell, so people are unlikely to think that I am.

Challenging In Action, 3: Fear of Spiders

'It's a cobweb. That means a spider – 1 have to get out of the room.'

1 *Are there reasons for my having this worrying thought?* Yes! Cobwebs and spiders go together and I know that I can go to pieces if I see a spider.

2 *Are there reasons against my holding this thought?* Sometimes I have mistaken cracks and pieces of hair for cobwebs and I have recently had experiences of being able to cope with small spiders.

3 *What is the worst thing that could happen?* It could be a spider and I could become terrified and feel sick.

4 *How would I cope with this?* In the recent past, I have used controlled breathing and distraction which has helped me to calm down. I could also call Carl for support and, if the worst came to the worst, I could always run away.

5 *What is a more constructive way of viewing the situation?* This might or might not be a cobweb and that might or might not mean that there's a spider here. Even if there is a spider, it could be small enough for me to tolerate or I might be able to use some coping strategies to deal with the situation. Carl is only in the next room if I need him and even if he couldn't come to support me, I could simply leave this room – although that would be my last resort.'

Difficulties in Challenging

'Can it be as simple as that?'

These examples might make thought challenging seem simple. It's not simple: if it were, you would be doing it all the time and would not need to read this book. Like all other skills it comes with practice, and practice should begin when you are not feeling anxious so that you can be as objective as possible. Remember that it is difficult to challenge worrying thoughts when you are distressed, so don't be surprised if you have to start by keeping a thought diary (see Diary 3 on page 120 and challenging your worries after your anxiety has subsided. As you become more skilled, you will be able to work through the five questions quickly and challenging your worrying thoughts will become more automatic. Eventually you will be able to challenge your thoughts in the anxiety-provoking situation itself.

'I can't hold on to my worrying thoughts'

Do write down your thoughts, because thought management is more effective if you clearly spell out your worries. Anxious thoughts often come in the form of questions: 'What is going to happen, will I pass out?' or 'Are they thinking that I look foolish?' It is difficult to argue with a question, so turn it into a statement: 'I am worried that I will pass out,' or 'I am worried that they will think that I look foolish.' It is very likely that the same thought or the same types of thought will crop up again and again. The more often a worry occurs, the more opportunity you have to devise a way of challenging it.

'I can't hold on to the challenging statement'

Do write down your challenging statements in full, as they will have more impact if you spell them out and you will better develop the skill of thought challenging if you get into the habit of examining your worries thoroughly.

'It's taking too long to take effect'

Eventually, the rational response to worrying thought can become as automatic as the anxiety response is now. However, you should expect to have 'good' days and 'bad' days: we all do. There are going to be times when you are not feeling well, or feeling tired or just too distressed to put challenging into action in the stressful situation. Do not worry about this too! Try to use distraction as a way of coping with the anxiety and, when you are feeling calmer, think about the rational response to your worries and also try to understand why challenging was difficult for you on this occasion.

SUMMARY

1 Everyone has worrying thoughts and they only become a problem when they are not easily dismissed.
2 Worrying can develop into a cycle of increasing anxiety if irrational beliefs are not challenged.
3 With practice, you can challenge your worries. You can do this by asking yourself how real is your fear and then generating a rational statement in response to it.

12

Managing avoidance: Graded practice

My father always used to say that if you fell off a horse you should get on again as quickly as possible. He was right and that's what I've learnt to do. I've learnt to face my fear by taking it one step at a time and building up my confidence in the process. Sometimes this is a slow process, and sometimes it requires a lot of planning, but I always get there in the end.

As we saw in Part One of this book, there are many different fears or phobias: fears of heights, public speaking, arguments, travelling, animals, busy places . . . the list is endless. Avoidance or procrastination, more than any other behavior, will maintain worry, fear or anxiety, and this section is devoted to strategies for helping you to give up avoidance. Facing what you fear is the most important aspect of overcoming it.

Where possible, it is best to face the fear *at your own pace*, not taking on too much too soon. The technique of graded practice is designed to help you to do just that. Sometimes, however, you might have to respond to a challenge within a limited time; on these occasions the strategy of problem-solving (chapter 13) will help you to generate solutions. Procrastination can heighten anxiety and the section on assertiveness (chapter 14) will help you to face difficult interpersonal situations, while time management (chapter 15) will help you to deal with tasks which you might otherwise put off.

Before you start to develop the techniques to help you face your fear, it is advisable to have learnt how to deal with the unpleasant bodily sensations of anxiety and your worrying thoughts. These are the areas we have tackled in chapters 8–11. This will build up your confidence about coping in difficult situations.

Facing fear through graded practice

First you must understand your fear: you need to know exactly what frightens you. For example, you might say that you are afraid of spiders, but this could mean quite different things to two different people. One might be able to tolerate a medium-sized spider at the other side of the room, and only become frightened if that spider moved nearer, while the other would become panicky just looking at a picture of a small spider. In this instance, you need to ask yourself:

- What size of spider makes me feel anxious?
- How near can I tolerate the spider?

- Does it make a difference where I am, or what time of day it happens to be?
- Does it make a difference if I am with someone?

When you have answered these questions, you will be able to describe your fear in more detail. You might discover that your anxiety is only triggered by large spiders, and that you can tolerate medium-sized or small ones; that you cannot bear a large spider in the same room as yourself, but you are reasonably comfortable if you know one is in another room; that you are more afraid of spiders at night, when you can't see them; and that you feel much less anxious when you have someone with you.

Another example could be a fear of shopping. This is a rather vague description and so, if you have this type of fear, you need to ask yourself questions such as:

- Which shops make me particularly anxious?
- What time of the day is worse or better for me?
- What makes it easier or harder for me to cope?

You might then redescribe your problem as being 'a fear of large supermarkets (but not small shops) which is worse during the busy times of the day'. You might also add that you find it easier to shop if you have a friend with you, and if you have planned your shopping trip thoroughly beforehand.

A further example might be a fear of public speaking. Again, this is a very general description, so you would need to ask yourself.

- What settings make me particularly anxious?
- What sort of audience or subject matter disturbs me most?
- What makes it easier or harder for me to cope?

You might discover that your problem is 'a fear of speaking in front of an audience of a dozen or so in a semi-formal setting'. You might find that you are not fearful of small, informal discussions or of large, very formal lectures when you read from a script. You might also realize that it is more difficult for you if you are already stressed – when you are abroad, for example, or very tired. You might find it easier if you have a colleague sharing the responsibility and if you have planned your presentation thoroughly beforehand.

By asking yourself these sorts of questions for each of your fears, you will be able to describe your problem in sufficient detail for you then to devise a plan of *graded* exposure to the difficult situation. This means facing the fear one step at a time by changing one aspect of your feared situation at a time. You may have more than one specific fear; if so, do this exercise for each of your fears. The first step is to describe your fear accurately: Figure 12.1 provides a space for you to write it down.

My Fear: _____

_____

_____

_____

Figure 12.1 Accurately describing your fear

Although the notion of facing your fear might seem alarming, you can learn to do it gradually, so that you never need feel very afraid. Graded practice helps you to overcome your fear by providing you with the opportunity to learn that certain situations or objects are not really dangerous, thereby building up your confidence. Practising in the situation that makes you feel uncomfortable or frightened actually reduces anxiety in the longer term – as long as the practice tasks are organized to lead you up to success. Attempt something relatively easy at first, and then gradually move on to more challenging situations at your own pace. In this way, you will build on success and increase your confidence.

There are three stages in graded practice:

- setting targets;
- grading tasks;
- practising.

Setting targets

Take your description of objects or situations you avoid or which make you very anxious. Remember to be very specific in describing your fears. If you have several, compile a list, arranging your fears in order of difficulty. These are your targets.

You might end up with a target list something like that shown in Figure 12.2.

Most difficult

1   Shopping in the hypermarket, alone, on Friday evening, when it is most busy.

2   Taking the bus from home into town (four miles), alone, in the morning when the bus is crowded.

3   Using the elevator at work (from the bottom floor to level seven) when there is nobody around.

Least difficult

4   *Sitting in the centre of the row at a movie or in a theatre, with my partner.*

Figure 12.2   Making a list of targets

Only list targets that you want to achieve, as these will be the ones you are most motivated to tackle. You don't have to take on every target which presents a challenge, only those that are relevant to you. For example, you might well be frightened by the idea of walking a tightrope, but if it does not make a difference to your life or you really don't want to walk a tightrope, you don't have to make it a target just because it is frightening.

When you have your targets ranked according to difficulty, select the easiest one to start with. However, if one of the targets is particularly urgent, you might have to begin with that one instead. At this stage, you should only tackle one target at a time. You will then need to work out a way of achieving this target in small, safe, graded steps or tasks.

Grading the tasks

Grading the tasks requires you to plan a series of small, specific steps of increasing difficulty, which culminate in achieving your target. The first task has to be manageable, so ask yourself, 'Can I imagine myself doing this with a bit of effort?' If you answer 'No,' then make the task easier. It is essential that you do not take risks: the aim of graded practice is to build on a series of successes, so you have to plan for success. In describing your fear, you asked yourself the question: 'What makes it easier for me?' Now you can incorporate as many of these factors as possible in order to increase the likelihood that the earlier tasks will be manageable. Later, you can increase the difficulty of the tasks so that you ensure that you build up your self-confidence.

For example, in the early stages of tackling a fear of shopping, you might find it easier to go with a friend, at a quiet time. If you were to continue to use your friend and to avoid busy times, you would not overcome your fear of shopping alone, but it is an ideal starting point for going on to develop greater independence.

Each task should be described in detail, as for example in Figure 12.3.

TARGET
Shopping in the hypermarket, alone, on Friday evening.

Tasks
1 Shopping in the local store, with my friend Bill, on Thursday afternoon, when it is quiet. Buying just one item, which I can pick up easily and take to the shopkeeper. I will have the correct money in my hand.
2 I'll repeat step one but I'll buy three items which I can pick up easily and pay by credit card so that I have to wait for the transaction.
3 This time I will buy at least ten items from a shopping list and pay by credit card.

Figure 12.3 Formulating tasks for each target

This is the starting point for graded practice; the tasks could develop in various ways before reaching the target. For example, this person could start to shop on her own and build on that, or could begin to take on larger stores, or could start shopping at busier times. Only one aspect of the task should be changed at a time and the choice of task would depend on what was most manageable and on practical constraints. For example, if Bill were only available for a short time, this person would try to become independent of him before changing the task to a busier time or a larger store. Each task presents an opportunity to use your coping skills (relaxation, controlled breathing, distraction, challenging).

In summary, the rest of the graded practice begun in Figure 12.3 might look like Figure 12.4.

Tasks

4 Using the local store, at a quiet time on my own.

5 Using the local store, alone, at a medium-busy time.

6 Using the local store, alone, at the busiest time.

7 Using a mini-market, alone, at a quiet time.

8 Using a mini-market, alone, at a busy time.

9 Using the supermarket, alone, at a quiet time.

10 Using the supermarket, alone, at a busy time.

11 Using the hypermarket, alone, at a quiet time.

12 Using the hypermarket, alone, at a busy time.

Figure 12.4   Tasks building up to the target

Now try breaking down your target into small, specific tasks (Figure 12.5).

Practising

Rehearse each step, using your coping skills, until you can manage it without difficulty; then move on to the next task, and so on. Don't be put off by some feelings of anxiety – these are only natural, because you are learning to master anxiety instead of avoiding it. To be helpful, practice has to be:

- regular and frequent enough for the benefits not to be lost;
- rewarding – recognize your achievements and learn to praise yourself;
- repeated until the anxiety is no longer there.

Target

Tasks

1

2

3

4

5

6

Figure 12.5 Compiling a list of tasks building up to a target

Graded practice in action: Managing a spider phobia

I've always been scared of spiders and I became really worried that I'd pass this on to my children. So, I asked a friend to help me overcome my fears by making me face spiders. She wasn't spider-phobic and so she was able to catch a really big one and keep it in a jar for me to get used to. I soon realized that, as long as there was a choice, I would not go near that spider. That's why she surprised me one day by putting the thing right in front of me. I say surprised me, but it really terrified me and I burst into tears and my fear was greater than ever.

Next, I asked my doctor what I should do and she explained that I'd done the right thing in trying to face my fear, but that I could have gone about this in a much more gradual fashion. With her help, I described my fear very precisely and then we drew up a series of steps which culminated in my tolerating a spider in the corner of the room. She also taught me a relaxation exercise which I was to use to overcome my anxieties while I was carrying out the practice.

My fear: Being alone in a room with a large spider (with a diameter of more than 2 cm), particularly if I am in the bedroom in the dark.

Target: To sit in my living room, on my own, with a 2 cm spider somewhere loose in the room.

Step 1: With my friend, sitting in the living room with a 1 cm dead spider, in the corner. Tolerate this until my anxiety is low.
Step 2: With my friend, sitting in the living room with a 2 cm dead spider, in the corner. Tolerate this until my anxiety is low.
Step 3: With my friend, sitting in the living room with a 2 cm dead spider 2 m away. Tolerate this until my anxiety is low.

Step 4: With my friend, sitting in the living room with a 2 cm dead spider 1 m away. Tolerate this until my anxiety is low.

Step 5: With my friend, sitting in the living room with a 2 cm dead spider next to me. Tolerate this until my anxiety is low.

Step 6: With my friend, sitting in the living room with a 1 cm live spider in a jar in the corner. Tolerate this until my anxiety is low.

Step 7: With my friend, sitting in the living room with a 2 cm live spider in a jar in the corner. Tolerate this until my anxiety is low.

Step 8: With my friend, sitting in the living room with a 2 cm live spider in a jar 2 m away. Tolerate this until my anxiety is low.

Step 9: With my friend, sitting in the living room with a 2 cm live spider in a jar 1 m away. Tolerate this until my anxiety is low.

Step 10: With my friend, sitting in the living room with a 2 cm live spider in a jar next to me. Tolerate this until my anxiety is low.

Step 11: With my friend, sitting in the living room with a 2 cm live spider somewhere in the room. Tolerate this until my anxiety is low.

Step 12: Alone in the living room with a 2 cm live spider, somewhere in the room. Tolerate this until my anxiety is low.

I felt reassured by this gentler plan and, luckily, my friend was still willing to help me so we both practised the relaxation exercises and then began at step 1. The doctor had checked with me that this step was something that I felt that I could achieve and so it was no surprise that it seemed easy. We moved on to steps 2 and 3 in the same day. Step 4 was rather more taxing and I had to practise this a few times before I could relax myself;

and I did wonder if step 5 wasn't over-ambitious as we had to go over this many times: with hindsight, I should have put in an extra step somewhere between 4 and 5. In contrast, steps 6 and 7 seemed hardly necessary once I had learnt to tolerate the dead spider so close. Within a few weeks, I had reached the top of the hierarchy and the children are really pleased with me, which is the biggest reward.

Difficulties in using graded practice

'I can't keep going: I keep failing'

If you find that a task is too difficult, don't give up or feel that you have failed. Instead, look for ways of making the task easier – perhaps as two or three smaller steps. Expect set-backs from time to time – this is only natural – and, when it happens, think about your task. Did you over-estimate what you could do and make the task too difficult? Did you practise when you were feeling unwell or tired? Did you have other things on your mind so that you could not put enough effort into your practice? If you keep a record of your practice, you can more easily work out why you have difficulties on certain days.

'I'm not getting anywhere'

As you move up your hierarchy of tasks, it is all too easy to downgrade or fail to appreciate your progress. By keeping a diary (see Diary 3, p. 144 and end of book) you will create a record of your achievements and you can review this as a reminder of your progress.

Don't forget to give yourself credit for your achievements, no matter how small. Try not to downgrade your successes and try not to criticize yourself: encouragement works better. In this way, you will manage to reach your goals and face your fears with confidence.

Diary 4 Achievement record

Date	Task	Anxiety rating (1–10)	Other relevant information

SUMMARY

1 Everyone has different fears: get to know just what your fears are and describe them very specifically. These are your targets.
2 Rank the targets in order of ease or priority. Take the first one.
3 Reduce the target to a series of achievable steps. Take no risks – you are planning to build on success.
4 Practise each step regularly and reward yourself each time you master your task.

13

Managing avoidance: Problem-solving

I'm still no good at keeping really calm in a difficult situation, but at least I can now do something construc-tive in a crisis. Others think that I am calm because I always ask sensible questions, come up with lots of solu-tions and I am very structured in putting them into action. I'm amazed how much I can achieve, even when I'm upset, by simply following a problem-solving protocol. Knowing this keeps my anxieties in check.

Graded practice is the best way of facing your fear if you have the time to organize a program for yourself. Sometimes, this isn't possible because a stressful event is imminent and you don't have time to follow a step-by-step approach. Occasions such as weddings, examinations or holidays tend to be fixed and we can suddenly find them almost upon us. Whatever the situation, being faced with an immediate problem can trigger panic and then it becomes even more difficult to plan how to cope. You might be confronted by a wholly unexpected event, or you may have to tackle some-thing that you have faced in the past but now find that you have little time to prepare for.

The problem-solving approach can help you to organize and focus your thinking so that you devise solutions to your dilemma rather than panic in the face of it. There are six steps in problem-solving:

- defining the problem;
- listing solutions;
- evaluating the pros and cons of the solutions;
- choosing a solution and planning to put it into action;
- doing it;
- reviewing the outcome.

Define the problem

Be specific about the task ahead and try not to confuse several tasks. Where possible, distinguish the different aspects of your problem and separate it into a collection of more manageable tasks, then make a plan for each. For example, an imminent wedding might give rise to the following worry:

I have to attend Mary's wedding next week and stand beside her as her best friend. Afterwards, I'll have to go to a reception.

This might reflect several problems:

1 'I have to deal with my claustrophobia in the church. This means being able to stand behind Mary for at

least twenty minutes, in a confined space and without the support of my partner.'

2 'I have to cope with being a focus of attention for several hours, without having a panic attack.'

3 'I am expected to attend a reception of about fifty guests. This will last for three or four hours and will be in the marquee.'

Once you have defined your task(s), select one and ask yourself:

- What is going to happen?
- When will this happen?
- Who is involved?

Only work on one task – it is false economy to try to problem-solve more than one difficulty at a time. Select your task and state your goal in very specific terms. Example 1, below, reflects the third aspect of the wedding guest's problem, while example 2 focuses on a different type of difficulty.

Example 1: 'I have to go to Mary's wedding reception, alone, next Saturday.'

Example 2: 'I have to see my boss about a pay rise within two days or lose the chance of an increase in salary.'

List solutions

Think of as many ways of dealing with the problem as you can, without censoring your ideas. At this stage, you are aiming to generate a wide range of possible courses of action and you will slow down the process if you try to judge your responses. The more solutions you generate the better. Write down all your ideas, no matter how trivial or outrageous they might seem, as some of your 'trivial' or 'outrageous' solutions might turn out to be most useful. It might be helpful to put yourself in someone else's shoes and consider how that person would respond if asked to deal with your problem.

Problem-solving in action, 1

Problem

'I have to go to Mary's wedding reception, alone, next Saturday.'

Solutions

Send my apologies, with an explanation of my problem.

Take one tranquillizer to calm me.

Send my daughter in my place.

Recall how I coped at the last wedding and try to use these coping strategies again.

Plan 'escape routes' that I could use if I found my anxiety was too great during the reception.

Talk all my fears through with my friend – it puts things in perspective.

Ignore the invitation.

Problem-solving in action, 2

Problem
'I have to see my boss about a pay rise within two days or lose the chance of an increase in salary.'

Solutions
Quit to avoid the confrontation.
Ask a colleague how I might phrase my request.
Ask my friend to rehearse with me what I might say.
Have several lunchtime drinks to give me courage.
Prepare myself by relaxing before I see my boss.
Ask for a time extension so that I am better able to prepare.
Decide to keep quiet and miss the opportunity of a rise this year.

Evaluate the pros and cons of each solution

At this point, you need to consider each of your solutions and decide which will have to be rejected because of unsuitability or impossibility. Then reflect on the remainder and rank in order the solutions according to usefulness for you at this time.

Problem-solving in action, 1

Problem
'I have to go to Mary's wedding reception, alone, next Saturday.'
Reject
Ignore the invitation.
Send my daughter in my place.

Accept

1st: Recall how I coped at the last wedding and try to use these coping strategies again.

2nd: Talk all my fears through with my friend – it puts things in perspective.

3rd: Plan 'escape routes' that I could use if I found my anxiety was too great during the reception.

4th: Send my apologies, with an explanation of my problem.

5th: Take one tranquillizer to calm me.

Problem-solving in action, 2

Problem

'I have to see my boss about a pay rise within two days or lose the chance of an increase in salary.'

Reject

Quit to avoid the confrontation.

Have several lunchtime drinks to give me courage.

Accept

1st: Ask a colleague how I might phrase my request.

2nd: Ask my friend to rehearse with me what I might say.

3rd: Prepare myself by relaxing before I see my boss.

4th: Ask for a time extension so that I am better able to prepare.

5th: Decide to keep quiet and miss the opportunity of a rise this year.

Choosing a solution and planning to put it into action

When you have done this, simply take your first-choice solution and start to plan how to put it into action.

In very specific and concrete terms, decide how you are going to implement your chosen solution. Be sure to answer the following questions:

- What will be done?
- How will it be done?
- When will it be done?
- Who is involved?
- Where will it take place?
- What is my contingency plan?

A contingency plan is a back-up plan which you can put into operation if your task is more difficult than you anticipated or something unexpected turns up and prevents you from carrying through your original course of action. For example, you might carry the telephone number of a friend whom you can ring to collect you from the wedding, or to whom you could talk if you got nervous just before your interview with your boss.

Problem-solving in action, 1

Task

Recall how I coped at the last wedding and try to use these coping strategies again

'I will sit in my study, where I shan't be disturbed, and I will try to recall all the details of the last wedding I attended. I will then write down all the strategies that I can remember using to help me get through that reception. If I find that I cannot remember enough or if I am disturbed too often to be able to do this task, I will try solution 2.'

Problem-solving in action, 2

Task

Ask a colleague how I might phrase my request

'I will telephone Robert this evening and explain my situation, and I will ask him what he would say to his boss if he were to argue for a pay rise. I will wait until the kids are in bed because I don't want to be disturbed by them. If Robert is not helpful or is not at home, my back-up will be Rose, whom I will try next. If she is not able to help, I can try Jean.'

Where possible, rehearse dealing with your task, either in imagination or with someone who could role-play with you. Also, scan all your solutions to see if you might profitably combine them. For example, you might find that 'Asking my friend to rehearse with me what I might say' links very well with 'Preparing myself by relaxing before I see my boss'.

The next step is putting this into action.

Do it

Try out your solution, making sure that contingency plans are in place and that you are properly prepared both physically and mentally. Whether or not you regard your action as successful, review it and see what you can learn.

Review the outcome

If your solution works and is sufficient, congratulate yourself and remember this successful experience for the future. Ask yourself why it was successful: what did you learn about your strengths and needs?

If your solution does not solve your problem, try to understand why it didn't – perhaps you were over-ambitious, perhaps you were not feeling strong that day, perhaps you misjudged someone else's response to you. Whatever conclusion you reach, remember that *you did not fail*. Expect some disappointments, but commend yourself for having tried. Learn as much as you can from the experience and go back to your solution list and select the next one.

You can continue to return to your list of solutions as often as you need to. The more solutions you are able to generate, the greater will be your store of options.

Problem-solving is a useful technique when you find yourself in a situation which requires prompt action.

However, it is always better to plan well in advance if you can; so try not to put off thinking about a difficult task until the last moment.

Difficulties in using problem-solving

'My solution didn't work and I didn't know what to do!'

Remember how important it is to prepare thoroughly. Thorough brainstorming is essential to problem-solving; without this, you will be short of solutions and contingency plans. When you do make specific plans for action, always ask yourself what could go wrong and prepare a back-up solution. If you do this, you should be able to devise a coping plan even if your chosen solution doesn't work.

'I can't possibly include such unhelpful solutions as avoidance and using drugs'

Why not? If the time isn't right for you to tackle the problem head-on, it is perfectly acceptable for you to use a compromise solution. If you have tried other ways of coping before resorting to your 'unhelpful' solution, accept that you have tried your best. Sometimes we all have to handle difficulties in ways which aren't entirely satisfactory to us. With time and practice in dealing with problem situations, you will be better able to use strategies with which you are happier.

SUMMARY

1 When a problem is immediate, you can tackle it by using a structured 'problem-solving' approach.

2 This involves six steps: defining the problem; listing solutions; evaluating the pros and cons of the solutions; choosing a solution and planning to implement it; implementing your chosen solution; evaluating your performance.

3 If your chosen solution does not work, choose another from your list and repeat the six steps. Be prepared to compromise.

14

Being assertive

It was a bit of a joke to others – I was either a mouse or a raging bull. I could not seem to get the balance right in confrontations and, as a result, I never achieved what I wanted. Assertiveness training helped me to find a position which was neither mouse-like nor bullish, and the more I practised achieving a stance which was not extreme, the easier it became. I found that I could do this even when I was upset and so my job became more enjoyable and the workers around me relaxed because they could trust me to be fair.

Assertiveness is another skill which can help you to manage worry, fear and anxiety. It describes a way of communicating your needs, feelings or rights to others without infringing their rights, and so it is particularly useful in dealing with interpersonal stresses.

Some find it difficult to be assertive because they do not recognize their basic entitlements, which would include the right to:

- ask a person for what you want;
- say 'No' without feeling guilty;
- have opinions, feelings and emotions;
- make your own decisions and cope with the consequences;
- choose whether or not to get involved in the problems of someone else;
- not to know about something and not to understand;
- make mistakes;
- be successful;
- change your mind;
- be private;
- be independent;
- change.

In learning to be assertive you will develop the ability to communicate these rights in a way that is clear and respectful of yourself and of others. This means not being passive, nor aggressive, nor manipulative, as these positions are not mutually respectful.

- The *passive* type of person opts out of conflict, can't make decisions and aims always to please others. This can be a very frustrating position because the passive person never respects her or his own needs.

At best, this could leave the person disappointed, and at worst s/he would feel resentful and thwarted.

- The *aggressive* type appears loud and forceful, belittling the thoughts, actions and personal qualities of others. He or she must win, has no time for the feelings or rights of others and has no reservation about behaving selfishly and attacking unfairly. At best, the aggressive person gets what s/he wants but can hurt others and damage relationships in the process.
- The *manipulative* type is indirectly aggressive and controlling. In this case, the attack is concealed. Thus, this person may *appear* to be supportive and understanding, but s/he will use emotional blackmail and will subtly undermine the other person in order to achieve a selfish goal
- The *assertive* type, by contrast to all the other types, sees both sides of a situation and recognizes the rights and needs of all parties. S/he takes responsibility for his or her own actions and does not need to put down others in order to feel comfortable.

The goal of assertive behavior is to confront without undermining oneself or others, whereas the goal of passive behavior is to avoid conflict and the goal of aggressive or manipulative behavior is to win. Passivity and aggression are easy to spot, while the manipulative person is less easy to recognize as an aggressor.

Asserting yourself

In preparing to be assertive you need to follow five steps:

- Decide what you *want*: this reflects your rights.
- Decide if it is *fair*, this reflects the other person's rights.
- Ask for it *clearly*.
- Be prepared to take *risks*.
- Keep *calm*.

You will find it easier to be assertive if you draw on your other stress management skills, which will help you to keep physically and mentally calm. You will also find it helpful to:

- *Prepare yourself*: brief yourself so that you know that your arguments are sound. Your argument does not have to be elaborate to be sound: simple explanations and requests can be effective. Script your argument in advance and organize it in terms of the *explanation*, your *feelings*, your *needs* and the *consequences*. See Figure 14.1 for an example. It can be useful to draft a script for yourself, so that you can rehearse your arguments in advance. Try them out on a friend if necessary. The more confident you are, the more effective you will be in confrontation.

The explanation: 'I want to discuss a problem with you. In the last few weeks, your children have been playing ball near to my fence and the ball often comes into my garden. In reclaiming the ball, they often damage my flowers.'

Your feelings: 'Although I realize that they are not doing this on purpose and that they need to play, I am tired of arriving home to find the garden trampled.'

Your needs: 'Therefore, I would appreciate it if you had a word with them, asking them to play elsewhere.'

The consequences: 'Otherwise I will have to tackle them about it.'

Figure 14.1   Being assertive: the four key points

- *Be positive*: a safe way of beginning is by using a compliment or a positive statement. For example, 'This is an excellent piece of work, but I would like you to write more clearly so that it is easier for me to read next time.' 'That is a very good idea, but I don't think that it would work here.'
- *Be objective*: do not get involved in personal criticism, but do explain the situation as you see it. Never criticize the person, only the behavior.
- *Be brief*: in order to avoid the other person switching off, butting in or side-tracking, be succinct. Don't theorize, just describe the facts.
- *Be aware of manipulative criticism*: don't expect that others will always be cooperative and concede your point. Although you might get an agreement, this is not inevitably the case.

The other person could try to distract you and undermine your efforts by using manipulative criticism. This either masquerades as caring or takes the form of frank criticism.

Dealing with manipulative criticism

Imagine that you had asserted that your boss gave you too much work to do. You had thought this through and discussed it with a friend, and, although you recognized that the department was very busy, you still felt that you were being unreasonably burdened. Your boss, rather than respecting your statement, reacts by using manipulative criticism such as:

Nagging   'Never mind that, haven't you finished yet? Your problem is that you are too slow. Now get on with the job.'

Caring   'That's all very well, but I really do think that it is in your best interest to improve your skills by carrying a substantial workload.'

Lecturing   'Well, quite *obviously* the real problem is . . . and you should . . .'

Insults   'Typical woman: can't cope in the real world.'

Concern   'If you are having these problems, are you sure you're right for this job, after all?'

Advice   'Let me tell you what I would do if I were you . . .'

Expert advice 'Believe me, I know what sort of a person you are and what's best for you, so you should . . .

Hurt You've made me feel terrible . . .

Each of these responses is aimed at undermining your needs and your rights and deflecting your argument. To deal with this, you will need to develop skills in standing your ground. There are two particularly useful approaches that will help you to be more assertive and handle manipulative criticism: the 'broken record' and fielding criticism.

The broken record

An unassertive person takes 'No' for an answer far too easily and is not persistent in making a point. A basic assertiveness skill is being persistent and repeating what you want over and over again – calmly. Once you have decided that what you want to say is fair, go ahead and assert it. Repeat your message until the other person gives way or agrees to negotiate with you.

This is a particularly useful approach when dealing with situations where your rights are clearly in danger of being abused, or where you are likely to be diverted by articulate but irrelevant arguments, or where you feel vulnerable because you know the other person will use criticism to undermine your self-esteem.

Once you have prepared your 'script' you can relax and repeat your argument. You know exactly what you are going to say, however abusive or manipulative the other person tries to be.

Fielding criticism

This is particularly helpful in dealing with manipulative criticism which might otherwise leave you feeling so badly about yourself that you agree to do something you would rather not do. There is often an element of truth in what is being said, but it is exaggerated. For example: 'Typical! You're always late . . . insensitive . . . selfish . . . expect others to do your work . . .' might well trigger some guilt and a subsequent unassertive response. In fact, the only truth in the statement might be, 'You are late'.

You can field criticism by calmly acknowledging that there may be some truth in what has been said. It can be left at that, if you do not want to get into a dialogue; or you may follow up with an assertion of your view, if you still have a point to make. Fielding also keeps the situation calm and allows you some time to think clearly. For example, when your boss yells: 'A typical woman: can't cope in the real world!' You might respond, 'That's right. I can't cope and that is why I am asking you to recognize that you give me too much to do.' When he says: 'Never mind that, haven't you finished yet? Your problem is that you are too slow. Now get on with the job,' you might respond with: 'You are right, I am too slow, given the amount of work that I have to deal with and that is why I am asking you to recognize that you give me too much to do.' When he says: 'You've made me feel terrible . . .', you might reply: 'I am sorry that you feel terrible but I still want you to recognize that you give me too much to do.'

Negative assertion

This is another means of avoiding being undermined by manipulative criticism. It requires you to agree calmly with the true criticism of your negative qualities. If someone says: 'Your appearance is a disgrace. You are so untidy and should be ashamed of yourself,' you might reply: 'Yes, I could be neater.' If you are able to accept yourself with all your faults, then your acknowledgment of them will not distress you and should put an end to your attacker's remarks.

Negative enquiry

This is the most difficult of the criticism-fielding strategies. It involves encouraging criticism so that you can decide whether your critic is genuine or engaging in manipulation. For example, your workmate might say: 'I wouldn't go for that job if I were you, you're far too diffident.' You could reply: 'In what ways do you think that I am diffident?' A manipulator might then be hard pressed to justify the statement, while a genuinely concerned colleague could elaborate. Once you have established your critic's real intentions, you can deal with the situation appropriately.

Negotiating

The aim of being assertive is not to win at all costs, but to reach a solution that is reasonable to all parties. This will involve compromise and negotiation. Negotiating can be made easier if you:

- ask for *clarification* of the argument so that you understand the issue and are aware of the other person's position, reasoning and needs;
- *keep calm* by using controlled breathing and adopting a relaxed attitude;
- *are prepared:* if you have time, do your homework – get the facts to support your case and rehearse your script;
- *acknowledge the other side of the argument* ('I understand your position, but . . .); try to empathize;
- *never attack* the whole person, only the behavior with which you disagree;
- *keep to the point:* don't get led away from your argument: make your point and repeat yourself as often as is necessary;
- are prepared to *take risks* and to *compromise*. Do not be stubborn and determined to win at all costs: this is aggressive! Decide in advance how far you are prepared to compromise.

Being assertive isn't very difficult once you are aware of, and have practised, these strategies. However, while you are a novice it is crucial to plan and rehearse, otherwise you will slip too easily into the position of aggressor, manipulator or passive avoider.

Remember that assertiveness is a skill and it improves with training and practice. You might find that it can be most effectively learnt in a class. See if there are assertiveness training classes in your area.

Assertiveness in action: Managing social phobia

I stopped being able to mix with others after a bus driver humiliated me because I didn't have the right money for my ticket. I was already feeling fragile after a row with my husband and I was completely unprepared for the hostility of the driver. Right in front of twenty passengers, he called me names and finally yelled: 'Get the right money or get off the bus. Now!' I just stood by the side of the road crying as the bus drove away.

The next day, I avoided using the bus and I walked into town. I was still upset and anxious so when an assistant in the delicatessen was brusque with me, I simply fled without finishing my shopping. After that I stopped going out alone.

Fortunately, I found a local assertiveness training class which helped me to learn that I could regain my confidence – as long as I remembered to prepare myself. I made a list of difficult situations, decided what I wanted from them and how to ask for this. I started with the easiest and worked my way up to taking a bus into town. On the day that I tackled that task, I really did not have the correct money for the fare. I thought about it and decided that it was reasonable for me to ask for a ticket anyway. I prepared my speech: 'I realize that you ask passengers to have the correct money for the fare, but I have been unable to find it today. I appreciate that you might not be able to give me change, but if you could, I would be very grateful.' I had also prepared myself in case the driver was hostile; I had planned to say: 'I made a reasonable request and I am sorry that you haven't respected that. I am perfectly prepared to walk but shall now have to report your conduct to the director of the bus company.' I practised these phrases until I felt confident with them.

In the end it all went smoothly and the driver let me travel without a fuss! Once I'd tackled that situation my old confidence started to return.

Difficulties in being assertive

'I get too nervous at the last minute'

It is not unusual to feel anxious when you are about to tackle a difficult situation, although there are steps you can take in order to minimize your fear. It always helps to start with the least threatening and work up to the most difficult challenges, developing your confidence as you go. It is most essential that you prepare yourself, rehearse and have a contingency plan for coping if things do not go smoothly.

'I have to back down: I can't achieve my goal'

The aim of being assertive is not to win (although this is often a welcome bonus) but to reach a reasonable conclusion. Good planning and practice will increase your chances of gaining the outcome you desire, but you should always be ready to compromise.

SUMMARY

1 Familiarize yourself with your basic rights.
2 Decide what you want or need and review this in the context of your rights and the rights of others.
3 Rehearse your arguments.
4 Be prepared to have to repeat yourself, field criticism and negotiate.

15

Time management

Time management reduced my stress and my worries by helping me to find enough time in the day to do what was necessary. At first, I had to invest some time in planning and organizing myself, but now things run smoothly and I find that I am less pressured and frustrated with my work and I can enjoy my family more. I feel as though I have a good balance in my life and that helps me to relax and to keep things in perspective.

Procrastination and poor organization can be a source of stress, and learning to manage time efficiently would reduce certain stress-related problems for many people. Time management is not complex: it's very straightforward, but it requires a great deal of organization and good preparation. Difficulties arise when the groundwork for time management is neglected.

The groundwork

You need some basic information about yourself and your routine before you can begin to reorganize your time, as you will need to balance your strengths, needs, priorities and goals with the demands on your time. You will need to address:

- the way you work;
- your routine;
- your priorities;
- reasonable goals.

The way you work

Review the way in which you work, exploring your strengths and your needs. For example, are you the sort of person who

Plans ahead?
Prioritizes?
Is able to focus your concentration?
Is punctual?
Puts things off?
Is obsessional?
Makes lists?
Works on a cluttered desk?
Can say 'No'?
Conforms/innovates?
Is able to delegate?
Prefers to work alone?

Reflecting on such questions, you might conclude that your strengths are that you are an innovator and forward planner with much energy and drive; however, you are untidy and disorganized and you need to have diaries and wall charts around to keep you mentally organized. You might also realize that, in order to work well, you need others around you to bounce ideas off and to give you inspiration – and so on.

What do you see as your strengths and needs? List them opposite each other (Figure 15.1).

Strengths	Needs

Figure 15.1 Listing strengths and needs

Your routine

You cannot manage time effectively until you know how you use it at present. The best way to find out is by keeping a record of your use of time which you can then analyze. By reviewing your time diary, you will get an indication of where and when you use time productively, when you waste time and where you can make savings. No one form of diary will suit everyone and you will need to tailor one to suit you. There are three basic ideas for time diaries:

- Listing your activities over set periods of time during the day. For example, you might break the day into 60-minute periods and record how you spent that hour at the end of each period (see Figure 15.2(a)).
- Listing everything that you do, with a note of the start time and how long it takes (including interruptions and changes of task). A list of activities might include dealing with mail, answering the telephone, writing letters, etc. (see Figure 15.2(b)).
- Listing the tasks which you habitually perform and logging the amount of time you spend on each (see figure 15.2(c)).

Figure 15.2   Examples of time diaries

(a)

9.00 a.m.	Cleared away breakfast dishes, washed them and sat with cup of coffee, making a shopping list. Began to read a new novel.
10.00 a.m.	Reading the novel instead of getting on with chores!
11.00 a.m.	Into the village to pick up the groceries and some wallpaper stripper.
12.00 noon	At home. Start to strip wallpaper in the children's room but change mind and begin to wash and rub down the paintwork instead. Run out of sandpaper so go into village to buy some more.
1.00 p.m.	Run into Rose and have lunch in the café instead of going home.

(b)

Task	Time began	Time finished	Time taken
Answer phone when I arrive in office	8.30	8.45	15 mins
Make coffee	8.45	8.50	5 mins
Talk with Suzie about her day's work (interrupted by secretary: 5 mins)	8.50	9.30	40 mins
Meeting with line manager	9.30	11.00	90 mins

(c)

My usual task	Total time taken on: Tuesday
1 Sorting bills	30 mins
2 Gardening	6 hours
3 Shopping	2 hours
4 Preparing meals	3 hours

The amount of detail that you put into your diary and whether or not you combine these formats depends on you and your requirements. As a rough guide, the worse your problem with time management, the more information you need in order to regain control. If you are recording paid employment, don't forget to log the time you spend on work when you are at home or the times when you slip into the office at weekends or in the evenings.

Although this sort of record keeping might seem laborious, you need only do it for a sample week or two and it is a wise investment of your time. Once you have your log, stand back and analyze it by asking questions such as:

- Do I have a healthy balance of work tasks?
- Am I carrying out my important tasks at the optimum time of day for me?
- Does my work day incorporate necessary breaks?
- Do I have time to plan? To review? To accommodate crisis?

Note where you could make useful changes to your daily routine. If you find it difficult to review your own record objectively, ask a friend for comments.

Your priorities

Now that you are familiar with your optimum way of working and ways in which you can make the most of your working time, you need to consider how to allocate time. This means reviewing all the important areas of your life: career, health, family, money and so on, and deciding how to prioritize each. For example, you might rank your family above health and health above money and career. In the light of this, you can begin to get your necessary tasks in perspective and allocate only a reasonable amount of time to each.

Unless you do this, you can find that you are poorly motivated or overstretched. For example, if you do not really prioritize tidiness and feel that it is more important to develop your interests or career, you are not going to be motivated to be tidy; if your family is more important to you than your business but you spend long hours in the office, you might feel frustrated because you are not spending time with your family and are overstretched when you do try to be with them. Yet it is not unusual for any of us to allocate time to tasks which we don't prioritize. As a consequence, we can be disappointed or frustrated and we are much less likely to do a good job.

It often helps to identify all the areas that are important to you and to rank them in order of personal priority. You can do this on the blank list provided in Figure 15.3.

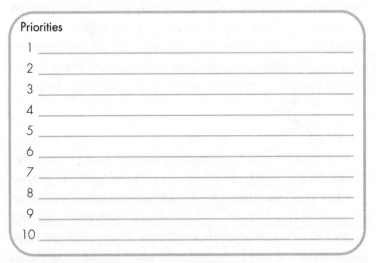

Priorities
1
2
3
4
5
6
7
8
9
10

Figure 15.3   Listing personal priorities

Do you allocate realistic amounts of time to your priorities? If not, perhaps you need to rethink and reorganize so that you give priority time to priority values. Unless you put your necessary tasks into the wider context of your personal priorities, you are creating a source of stress for yourself.

In prioritizing, it is crucial to be clear about your responsibilities. If you are unclear, you run the risk of taking on too much and/or letting down others and/or wasting your time. If you have a job description, get it out and check whether or not you are matching it. If you do not have a job description, ask yourself questions like: 'Is this my responsibility?' 'Is this reasonable?' 'Do I want to do this?' Are you prioritizing shopping for the person next door because it matters to you or because you can't say no? Are you taking on extra teaching because it is a work priority for you or because it is a priority for your boss? It might be helpful to review the previous chapter on assertiveness to help you limit the tasks you undertake to those which are reasonable or to those which you genuinely choose.

Goal Setting

Now you can reflect on your immediate and long-term goals to see how realistic they are, given your general characteristics and priorities. Do not undermine important areas of your life in pursuit of your goals, otherwise you will create stress for yourself. For example, if your current business venture is your first priority and you know that it is important for you to establish yourself within the next two years, do not undermine this by getting side-tracked into social commitments in order to please your friends. Later your goal might be to widen your social circle and take more leisure time with them. Learn to compromise and to rethink your goals regularly.

When defining your goal, remember that you need to be concrete. A vague or ambiguous notion of what you hope to achieve is a poor motivator. Also, if the goal is not clearly defined, it is difficult to appreciate when you have achieved it and you might not even realize that you have. Be specific: who, what, when, how much, must be spelt out clearly. For example, the goal 'to be a better timekeeper' is too vague. A more useful definition would be:

Goal: To arrive at the school, with the children, no later than 8.30 a.m. on quiet days and not later than 8.50 a.m. when I'm busy; to take a lunch break between 12.30 and 1.00 p.m., which should last at least 30 minutes; to leave work by 3.00 p.m. when I have a quiet day, but never later than 3.15 p.m., even when we are busy; to collect the children by 3.30 p.m. so that we can be home by 4.00 p.m.

This goal is unambiguous, so it is difficult to bend the rules and easy to appreciate when the goal has been achieved. The goal also recognizes personal needs for breaks during the day and flexibility.

Sometimes goals can be achieved in a single step: the revision of a diary can achieve several time management goals at once; one telephone call can allow you to delegate a series of tasks; a single interview can find you the au pair which will make a big difference to your stress levels.

However, some goals need more planning. Try to recognize when the attainment of a goal requires more than one step – if you don't, and you expect to reach your target by a single action, you will be disappointed. If a target seems overwhelming, you are very likely to procrastinate unless you reduce the goal to several manageable steps.

It might be helpful for you to think about your goals now, in the light of what you have discovered about your strengths, needs, routine and priorities.

Scheduling your time

When you have done the groundwork, you will be in a position to reschedule your use of time for greater efficiency. Be prepared to reorganize each day and allocate time for this, learning as much as you can from mistakes you have previously made in organizing your time. Don't be rigid in your forward planning, because from time to time you will have to act in response to a crisis or a sudden opportunity.

First, get yourself an organizer, such as a desk diary, a wall chart or a personal organizer – whatever best meets your requirements and personal style. Next, sort your goals into the long, medium and short term and list them. Long-term goals could cover six months or more; you can write in target completion dates as deadlines. Medium-term goals might be those which you can carry over to the next month, and short-term goals are those which need to be tackled this week. Make a review time for each list so that you can reassess and re-evaluate your progress, update your values and priorities, and plan for further goal attainment.

Once you have a system like this in operation you will find that it takes little time to organize – but you *must* make available organization time each day. And you *must* budget for monthly review. If you don't, the system breaks down.

Daily time management

Certain aspects of time analysis should be carried out each day; with practice, this can become part of your daily routine. Each day you will need to generate a 'To do' list of tasks which have been prioritized (A-D) according to the criteria.

- A: must do today;
- B: should do today;
- C: could put off;
- D: delegate.

This involves more lists but is worthwhile because it can save you time. Delegation is fundamental to time management, and we will deal with delegation next.

Make sure to review how effectively you managed time at the end of each day, as this exercise yields useful information. If you did not achieve your objectives for the day, ask yourself why and then ask yourself what can be learnt from this. Did you fall short of your objective because you underestimated your workload? If so, how might you replan? Did you not meet your day's goals because you were not able to say 'No' to interruptions? If so, you might try an assertiveness training course. Did you lose time because your work environment is badly organized and you can't get hold of things as you need them? If so, try rearranging your office.

You can further increase your efficiency by learning to plan and problem-solve (see Part Two, chapter 13) and by learning to delegate.

Delegation

Few of us can manage to do everything ourselves, and it is often unnecessary to expect to do so. Many tasks can be delegated and this is fundamental to using time wisely. It might mean giving up some enjoyable jobs, but to be effective under time pressure you have to limit yourself to appropriate work. It *isn't* faster to do everything yourself, and although training someone might take up time right now, it will pay off in the future. Delegating requires you to:

- Identify the task to be delegated.
- Identify to whom it should be given. The task must be suitable for the person who is to take it on: it is no good asking your five-year-old son to wash and dress himself in his school uniform if he is not yet able to button buttons and tie laces; it might be unwise to entrust your secretary with the task of typing your business letters in French if she does not know the language.
- Brief the relevant person(s) and *train* them by close supervision, with *gradual withdrawal* ending with *monitoring* of progress.

Training, gradual withdrawal and monitoring are emphasized because delegation will fail if the delegate is not supervised and paced appropriately, and the standard of the delegated task can deteriorate if progress is not monitored. You need to budget for review time with the person to whom you delegate, whether this is an executive, a spouse, a child or a student.

Delegation is different from simply telling someone what to do, and will fail if the person to whom you delegate is not also given the authority to carry out the task with minimum need for your intervention. If you delegate a job to your small son, you will have to accept his mistakes; and if you give a worker a task, you will have to be able to stand back and risk that person making errors. Error can be minimized by good training and supervision; but in delegating you should be giving over *responsibility with authority*, even if you still retain overall legal responsibility or accountability.

It is also important to remember that delegation is not an excuse for passing on all the boring or unrewarding tasks. Others need fulfilment and challenge if they are to cooperate and to develop in their own right.

Time management in action: Managing burn-out

The stress crept up on me over several months. My department received more and more requests and I was really excited by this. I realized at the time that I was working at the expense of my home life, but I thought that this was only temporary and I really loved being in such demand. The reputation of my department was so important to me that I made sure that I was involved in every project and I even revised colleagues' work because I didn't feel that it was up to my standards. My partner warned me that I was working too hard but I didn't pay too much attention. Then I got the chest pains. They were so severe that I thought that I was having a heart attack. My doctor said that they were stress-related and if I didn't change my work hours, I could put my health at risk.

So I had no choice but to review how I worked. The first step was accepting that I must work less than a ten-hour day. I was worried that I'd find life dull without my work projects, so my partner and I planned to do much more together when I came home. Working fewer hours meant that I did need to use my time more effectively and so I asked our personnel officer to send me on one of the firm's time management courses. It was a few hours well spent. Within the week, I had reorganized my work day so that I no longer wasted time doing jobs that others could manage better and I stopped floating from project to project in an unproductive way, focusing my energy instead on the most important ones for me. I had to overcome my reservations about delegating – but my health was more important and delegating turned out to be the most useful thing I did.

I learnt, to my surprise, that I produced more in less time once I became better organized, and I also discovered that there is more to life than work – for which I am very grateful.

Difficulties in using time management

'I haven't the time!'

This must be the most common stumbling block to using time management strategies. It's true it does take time to organize yourself, but this is an investment for later.

'It's no good: it doesn't work for me'

This is most likely to reflect poor planning and not giving enough time to the task of analysis and reorganization. Don't compromise by reorganizing your use of time half-heartedly. Also, you need to allow time for your new system to become accepted by those around you. Others may have to make adjustments as you delegate or as you give less attention to them, and some might even rebel. Accept that there might be a period of settling in.

'I can't delegate'

Among the most common objections to delegating are: 'It's easier/faster to do it myself'; 'If you want a good job doing, do it yourself'; 'I haven't the time to show her how to do it'; 'He couldn't manage it'; 'She wouldn't do it properly'; 'At the end of the day, I'm responsible'. Think now about ways in which you can challenge such statements, and when you find yourself using them, consider how justifiable your objections really are.

SUMMARY

1 The following are fundamental to good organization:
    knowing your strengths and needs;
    knowing your routine;
    knowing your priorities;
    knowing how to set reasonable goals.
2 In order to manage time effectively, you need to devise a workable system for yourself which meets *your* needs and which you review and revise regularly.
3 Good time management involves delegating those tasks for which it is appropriate to give responsibility to others. Authority to carry out the task must also be given to the delegatee.

16

Getting a better night's sleep

Once I had fallen into the pattern of exhausting day and sleepless night followed by another stressful day, I couldn't break out of it. I felt trapped and frustrated. I felt ill and tired and I thought that I would never cope again. Discovering how to break the pattern gave me back a sense of control over my life and I began to feel like my old self again.

Sleep problems are common, with as many as one in five people complaining of difficulty in dropping off to sleep, of waking too frequently during the night or of waking too early in the morning. It is quite normal not to have a solid night's sleep. Delay in falling asleep and waking up early only become a problem when you worry about them, because worry, more than anything, will interfere with your sleep. Worrying about not sleeping can be more uncomfortable and tiring than the lack of sleep itself. Lying awake when you want to be asleep is unpleasant and can leave you feeling exhausted the next day.

Some facts about sleep which might ease your concerns are:

- There is no such thing as the ideal length of sleep: some people need ten hours and some three. If you sleep fewer than eight hours a night, you are not necessarily depriving your body – you might not need eight hours. Your best indicator of need is how you feel after different periods of sleep.
- As you get older, you need less sleep.
- Everyone has 'broken' sleep. We all wake several times during the night and simply go back to sleep, often without registering the waking. It is only when you worry about waking that you will notice it, and then this worrying can keep you awake.
- It is not harmful to lose a few 'good' nights' sleep. Everyone has the odd period of poor sleep, especially when under stress. The only ill effect of this is that you will feel tired during the day and might find yourself more irritable or less able to cope with things. Once your sleep pattern is restored, you will feel fine again.
- Sleep is affected by many things – stress, mood, exercise, food, medicines, alcohol. By modifying some of these things, you can take control of your sleeping pattern without resorting to sleeping medication.

Why avoid medication?

The simple answer to this question is that sleeping tablets are not helpful in the long term and are often addictive.

An occasional sleeping pill, taken on your doctor's advice, might be useful in a crisis, for example, but your body can begin to rely on them and it can then become difficult to sleep without medication. When you stop taking sleeping tablets, you can find that your sleep pattern is worse than ever and that you are tempted to go back on the tablets. This can be the beginning of a cycle of poor sleep and dependency on drugs. Fortunately, you can deal with sleep problems without resorting to medication, simply by changing your behavior.

Know your own sleep patterns

First, keep a sleep diary (see Diary 5, p. 190 and end of book) to find out more about your sleep patterns. All you need to do is fill in the following details for a week or two:

- The date and any event which might affect your sleep: e.g. what food you ate before going to bed, what level of stress you were under, what exercise you took, etc.
- How many hours of sleep you had and how many waking episodes you recalled.
- What you did when you could not sleep: e.g. made a cup of tea, read, looked at the ceiling.
- Whether or not this helped.
- How alert or awake you felt the next day. You could rate yourself on a 10-point scale where 1 means:

Diary 5 Sleep diary

Record the date and note any events which might affect your ability to sleep. For example, the food you ate before retiring, your stress levels, your activity just before going to bed, and so on. If you wake, note what you did to get back to sleep and whether or not this was helpful. Next day, note how many hours sleep you had and rate your level of alertness (Rating 1) and how well you performed during the day (Rating 2), using the following scales.

1. Alertness:

1	2	3	4	5	6	7	8	9	10

Not at all alert   Reasonably alert   Very alert

2. Performance:

1	2	3	4	5	6	7	8	9	10

Poor performance   Moderate performance   Performed well

Date	Notes	Waking episodes	Activity if not asleep: helpful Y/N	Hours sleep	Rating 1	Rating 2

'Felt as dull and sleepy as I can imagine', and 10 means: 'Felt fully alert and awake.'
- How well you carried out your work the next day, again using a 10-point scale.

When you have kept the diary for several nights, you will be able to see whether or not you have a problem. If you are feeling reasonably alert and working reasonably well on your usual number of hours' sleep, then you don't have a problem. If you are feeling tired and your work is suffering, then you can start to help yourself by trying the following suggestions.

Suggestions for a better night's sleep

- *Study your sleep diary*: is poor sleep linked with life stresses and therefore likely to improve as the stress eases? Are there particular behaviors associated with poor sleep you could change? Can you identify unhelpful ways of coping, such as watching TV in bed which keeps you awake? What helped you to go back to sleep? Try these things again, and avoid those which did not help.
- *Try to relax*: remember that no one has unbroken sleep and everyone has the odd period of poor sleep. If you don't worry, you will sleep better. Make time to relax an hour or two before you go to bed. For example, take a gentle stroll or a warm bath, or sit

and listen to soothing music. Use relaxation exercises and distraction exercises (see chapters 9 and 10) to keep your tension at a minimum when you are in bed.

- *Keep your daily stress low* by making sure that you are not overworking and that you are dealing with problems as they arise and not taking them to bed with you as worrying thoughts. You might consider getting the support of friends or a professional counsellor if you find it too difficult to deal with work stress or emotional problems by yourself.

- *Take exercise in the day.*

- *Avoid caffeine* (in chocolate, tea, coffee, cocoa and cola). Try having a warm milky drink before bed. Cut down on alcohol and nicotine at night: although these are sedative in small doses, alcohol becomes a stimulant as it is broken down and nicotine becomes a stimulant in larger doses. Avoid spicy food or a heavy meal in the evening, but do not go to bed hungry as this will keep you awake. Try having a light snack.

- *Make sure that your bedroom is quiet* and that your bed is comfortable, and empty your bladder before you try to go to sleep.

- *Go to bed only when you are sleepy*, and use your bed only for sleeping – not eating or reading or watching the television – until you have re-established a good sleep pattern. It is important that your bed becomes associated with sleep and not waking activities.

- *Get out of bed and do something else*: if you have not fallen asleep after fifteen to twenty minutes, or if you wake and do not go back to sleep. Do something simple and not too energetic, like light housework or reading, then try to sleep again. Keep repeating this until you do fall asleep rather than lie in bed tossing and turning, as that will tend to increase your agitation.
- *Wake at a regular time each day*: you will find that you sleep better if you have a regular routine. Set an alarm and get up when it goes off and don't be tempted to catch up on your sleep during the day or through 'sleep binges' at the weekends. For the time being, you are trying to establish a good sleep pattern.

If you follow these suggestions, and practise relaxation, you should have little difficulty in sleeping. If the problem does persist, particularly early morning wakening, then see your doctor for further advice.

Other sleep problems

From time to time, you might worry about other sleep-related experiences which are not harmful. For example:

- *Sleep paralysis* During some parts of sleep, our bodies are 'paralysed' so that we do not act out our dreams. Sometimes, on drowsing or waking, we can experience a very temporary episode of wakefulness without the ability to move. This can be frightening but it will last only a second or so.

- *Sensory shocks* These are harmless bodily sensations in the form of jerks or the sensation of falling which might be vivid enough to wake the sleeper.
- *Hallucinations* These can occur when a person is in a state of half-sleep or dozing or waking. They are normal and fleeting but can be vivid enough to be alarming.

None of these experiences is harmful and accepting them is the best way of dealing with them. However, *sleepwalking* can be dangerous and it is advisable to discuss this with a general practitioner or a specialist.

Sleep management in action

I thought that I was simply a light sleeper, that I could never expect to sleep as well as my wife. Then we took our dream holiday – not a few days away with my mobile phone and laptop computer to keep us company, but a real get-away-from-it-all vacation. We swam, we walked, we forgot work and I slept like a log.

Once we returned home, my sleep again became broken and I felt tired the next day. So we sat down and worked out how I could get a good night's sleep again. We realized that the things that had made a difference for me were: I did not worry about the business; I exercised and relaxed every day; and we ate and drank healthily. Now that I knew that it was possible for me to sleep well, I was very motivated to try to restore my holiday sleep pattern.

I gave up coffee and alcohol in the evenings: I left work in the very early evening so that we had time to do something relaxing each night – this might be going to the theatre, or hiring a video or playing a game of squash. On those evenings when I could not avoid working late, I made sure that I took a relaxing bath with a good book before going to bed – this way I could clear my mind of worries. I began to sleep better within days. I wish I'd done it sooner.

Difficulties in using sleep management

'I still have the odd night of poor sleep'

You can expect this to continue. We all have the occasional night when we don't sleep well and this should not impair our work or the quality of our lives. It is a good idea to note when you have a poor night's sleep so that you can learn what affects your sleep pattern.

'I still can't sleep for more than a few hours'

Study your sleep diary – do you function well on a few hours' sleep? If so, don't worry, just make the most of it. If you do not function well, revise your sleep programme: perhaps you need to include more active relaxation, or to cut down even more on stimulants, or develop better distraction techniques to keep your mind from worrying.

'I would sleep well if only my partner didn't keep waking me'

If your partner wakes you because s/he is a poor sleeper, direct her/him to this chapter. If your partner wakes you because of her or his disturbing behavior (sleepwalking, snoring, sensory shock, etc.), you might have to consider sleeping separately if you want a good night's sleep. Also, you could suggest your partner seek a doctor's help for such problems.

SUMMARY

1 Worry, more than anything, will interrupt your sleep.
2 Familiarize yourself with facts about sleep so that you do not worry unnecessarily.
3 Prepare yourself before going go bed: watch what you eat and drink, relax, don't lie awake in bed and don't 'catnap' during the day.

17

Coping in the long term

At first I thought that stress management was like taking antibiotics: take the course and feel better. Well, I did feel better, but stress management is a long-term commitment, rather like exercise: the more you prac-tise, the better you feel, but it won't always be plain sailing. I've learnt how to make stress management part of my life and I learnt how to predict and to handle the occasional setback. This isn't an onerous task, it's enjoyable and a wise investment of my time and effort.

So far, this book has aimed to help you to change your view of stress and to develop coping skills. This final chapter will explain how you can maintain your achievements so that worry, fear and anxiety need not be a problem in the future. The skills which you have now learnt will become easier to use and more effective with practice, but you must keep on practising.

You can further 'stress-proof' yourself by always plan-ning ahead, or 'blueprinting', and by learning to use set-backs to help you continue your progress. Changing your lifestyle to minimize stress will also help you to continue to build up your confidence. Finally, familiarizing yourself with how to cope with panic attacks should help you to feel more able to manage unforeseen crises.

'Blueprinting'

This is also known as 'troubleshooting'. It requires you to set aside some time for thinking about future challenges and identifying where and when you will be vulnerable to stress. You might list challenges like: 'Giving a brief presentation to colleagues about my work', or 'Taking this faulty iron back to the shop', or 'Going into the garden shed, which has spiders inside'. Try to identify your challenges for the next week or two and list them in Figure 17.1.

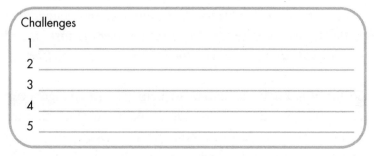

Challenges

1 _____
2 _____
3 _____
4 _____
5 _____

Figure 17.1   Identifying future challenges

Once you have predicted those situations that will be stressful for you, plan how you will deal with each challenge. Think how you might prepare yourself by relaxing and by rehearsing before you are in the situation, and then plan how you will deal with the stress when you face it.

Which of your coping techniques will help you? Consider how you will deal with the situation if everything does not go according to plan; have a back-up scheme.

If you anticipate difficult times and predict your needs during such periods, you can organize your life to mini-mize your distress and the risk of losing confidence. For example, if you know that Christmas pressures always cause stress and leave you feeling miserable and likely to turn to chocolate and alcohol for comfort, you could reorganize your Christmas activities to limit your stress. You might plan a holiday abroad; you could make sure that you did not have easy access to alcohol and chocolate; you could schedule time to yourself, you could practise saying 'No'. Look at your list and work out some plans for coping; make a note of these in Figure 17.2.

Coping with set-backs

Even the best laid plans can come unstuck, and on occa-sion you will be disappointed in your performance. This is a time of vulnerability to relapse. If you view a set-back or a disappointment as a 'failure', you will feel demoral-ized and this will begin to sap the confidence you have been building over the course of this program. If, however, you use a set-back as an opportunity for learning more about your strengths and needs, you can turn a disap-pointment to your advantage.

Each set-back tells you something about yourself and your vulnerability in a particular situation. If a woman had a disappointing shopping expedition she could leave it at

Challenge	Plan for coping
1	
2	
3	
4	
5	

Figure 17.2 Making plans for coping with future challenges

that – or she could consider as many explanations for the disappointment as possible. In reviewing the outing, she might realize that it was the first time she had tried shopping alone in a long time, that the crowds were so dense that she felt that she could not breathe, that the shop did not have what she wanted so she grew frustrated. She might also realize that her period began the next day. This would help her to plan her next shopping trip so that she increased the likelihood of success. For example, she might decide not to take on a major challenge when she was premenstrual; she might now appreciate the importance of not taking too big a step at once and arrange for a friend to accompany her next time; she could shop at a quieter time; and she might decide to telephone the shop to check that they had what she wanted so that she could avoid frustration.

It is important to:

- accept that slips, or setbacks, will happen: a *lapse* in your progress does not necessarily mean its *collapse*
- recognize that a setback is a chance to learn: use this knowledge to plan how to cope in the future.

Changing your lifestyle

There are simple modifications you can make to your day-to-day routines which will further 'stress-proof' you in the future.

- *Build a 'relaxation slot' into your daily routine.* This might only take a few minutes but it will be a valuable use of your time. Try to develop the habit of relaxing.

- *Do as many pleasurable things as possible*: if your pleasurable activities release tension too, so much the better. You might try physical exercise and yoga.
- *Don't let stress build up*. If something is worrying you, seek advice from friends or professionals. Find out now where you might seek help – have a list of useful telephone numbers that will include friends and organizations such as the Samaritans.
- *Organize yourself at home and at work*. If you need professional help, find a time management course in your area.
- *Assert yourself at home and at work*. Avoid the unnecessary stress of being a doormat or being exploited. Look out for local assertiveness training classes or search the library for books on this topic.
- *Avoid getting overtired or taking on too much work*. Recognize when you have reached your limit and stop. Take a break and try to do something relaxing and/or pleasurable.
- *Don't avoid what you fear*. If you find something is becoming difficult for you to face up to, don't back away – if you do, that situation will only grow more frightening. Instead, set yourself a series of small and safe steps to help you meet the challenge.
- *Remember to recognize your achievements* and to praise yourself. Never downgrade yourself and don't dwell on past difficulties. Give yourself credit for what you do achieve, plan and look ahead.

Coping with a panic attack

It is always easier to cope with anxiety in its early stages, and this is why it is helpful to recognize the onset of tension, and to use this as your cue for putting coping techniques into action. However, there may be times when you miss the early signs and you become panicky. At this point it is hard to think clearly and act sensibly, so it is important to have learnt what to do if you get extremely anxious or have a panic attack. If you are well prepared, you will be able to manage your feelings.

- Remember, *your feelings are normal and harmless*.
- Use *controlled breathing* to ease your discomfort.
- *Accept what is happening to you*. If you wait, the fear will pass; if you run away, it will be more difficult to cope with the situation in the future.
- *Control frightening thoughts*. Try to use distraction or to think of the situation in a more logical way.
- As soon as you are able, *make a plan* to ease the situation. You could rest until you feel calmer or get the help of a friend, for example. Whatever you decide, try to carry it out in a relaxed way.

SUMMARY

1 Coping in the long term requires regular practice of all that you have learnt.
2 Establish blueprints for the future.
3 Have plans for coping with set-backs.
4 Review your daily routine and consider changing your lifestyle to minimize stress.
5 Know how to manage a panic attack.

Postscript

For some, this self-help guide will be all that is needed to learn how to manage worries, fears and anxieties. However, others might find that they need more guidance in learning to deal with the problem. If this is the case, your medical practitioner should be able to offer support and/or specialist referral if necessary. If you should find that the exercises in Part Two are not sufficient, do not regard this as a failure but as an indication of the complexity of your needs. You might well have had the same experience if you were to teach yourself a foreign language. First, you would try learning from tapes and teach-yourself books; but, if your lifestyle or your learning style were not suited to self-teaching, or if you have trouble with languages, you might feel the need to join an evening class which would structure your learning. In this case, you probably would not view yourself as having failed. Nor have you 'failed' if you find that this program is more helpful if it is supplemented by a support group or some individual work with a specialist.

Scripts for making your own relaxation training tapes

Although many discover that relaxation training is an invaluable exercise in stress management, some do find that it is difficult to remember all the elements of each exercise and to pace the exercises properly. If you find that this is so, you can make your own instruction tapes by recording the scripts below. The aim of making the tape is to provide you with soothing instructions, so choose a time when you are feeling reasonably relaxed and your voice is not strained and you are not hurried. If you prefer the sound of a friend's voice, ask her or him to make the tape for you.

Exercise 1: Progressive muscular relaxation or deep relaxation

This exercise will help you to distinguish between tension and relaxation in your muscles, and teach you how to relax at will by working through various muscle groups first tensing and then relaxing them. Starting with your feet, you will work up through your body slowly and smoothly, letting the sensation of relaxation deepen at its own pace.

First, get as comfortable as you can . . . Lie flat on the floor with a pillow under your head, or snuggle in your chair . . . If you wear spectacles, remove them . . . Kick off your shoes and loosen any tight clothing . . . Relax your arms by your side and have your legs uncrossed. Close your eyes, and don't worry if they flicker – this is quite usual.

Instructions

'You are beginning to relax . . . Breathe out slowly . . . Now, breathe in smoothly and deeply . . . Now, breathe out slowly again, imagining yourself becoming heavier and heavier, sinking into the floor (or your chair) . . . Keep breathing rhythmically, and feel a sense of relief and of letting go . . . Try saying "relax" to yourself as you breathe out . . . Breathe like this for a few moments more . . .

(READ ONCE)

'Now, begin to tense and relax the muscles of your body . . . Think of your feet . . . Tense the muscles in your feet and ankles, curling your toes towards your head . . . Gently stretch your muscles . . . Feel the tension in your feet and ankles . . . Hold it . . . Now let go . . . Let your feet go limp and floppy . . . Feel the difference . . . Feel the tension draining away from your feet . . . Let your feet roll outwards and grow heavier and heavier . . . Imagine that they are so heavy that they are sinking into the floor . . . More and more relaxed . . . growing heavier and more relaxed . . .

(REPEAT)

'Now, think about your calves . . . Begin to tense the muscles in your lower legs . . . If you are sitting, lift your legs up and hold them in front of you, feeling the tension . . . Gently stretch the muscles . . . Feel that tension . . . Hold it . . . Now release . . . Let your feet touch the floor and let your legs go floppy and heavy . . . Feel the difference . . . Feel the tension leaving your legs, draining away from your calves . . . Leaving your calves feeling heavy . . . Draining away from your feet . . . Leaving them feeling heavy and limp . . . Imagine that your legs and feet are so heavy that they are sinking into the floor . . . They feel limp and relaxed . . . Growing more and more heavy and relaxed . . .

(REPEAT)

'Think about your thigh muscles . . . Tense them by pushing the tops of your legs together as hard as you can . . . Feel the tension building . . . Hold it . . . Now, let your legs fall apart . . . Feel the difference . . . Feel the tension draining away from your legs . . . They feel limp and heavy . . . Your thighs feel heavy . . . Your calves feel heavy . . . Your feet feel heavy . . . Imagine the tension draining away . . . Leaving your legs . . . Leaving them feeling limp and relaxed . . . Leaving them feeling so heavy that they are sinking into the floor or your chair . . . Let the feelings of relaxation spread up from your feet . . . Up through your legs . . . Relaxing your hips and lower back . . .

(REPEAT)

'Now tense the muscles of your hips, and lower back by squeezing your buttocks together . . . Arch your back, gently . . . Feel the tension . . . Hold the tension . . . Now let it go . . . Let your muscles relax . . . Feel your spine supported again . . . Feel the muscles relax . . . Deeper and deeper . . . More and more relaxed . . . Growing heavier and heavier . . . Your hips are relaxed . . . Your legs are relaxed . . . Your feet are heavy . . . Tension is draining away from your body . . .

(REPEAT)

'Tense your stomach and chest muscles, imagine that you are expecting a punch in the stomach and prepare yourself for the impact . . . Take in a breath, and as you do, pull in your stomach and feel the muscles tighten . . . Feel your chest muscles tighten and become rigid . . . Hold the tension . . . Now slowly breathe out and let go of the tension . . . Feel your stomach muscles relax . . . Feel the tightness leave your chest . . . As you breathe evenly and calmly, your chest and stomach should gently rise and fall . . . Allow your breathing to become rhythmic and relaxed . . .

(REPEAT)

'Now think about your hands and arms . . . Slowly curl your fingers into two tight fists . . . Feel the tension . . . Now hold your arms straight out in front of you, still clenching your fists . . . Feel the tension in your hands, your forearms and your upper arms . . . Hold it . . . Now, let go . . . Gently drop your arms by your side and imagine the tension draining away from your arms . . . Leaving your upper arms . . . Leaving your forearms . . . Draining away from your hands . . . Your arms feel heavy and floppy . . . Your arms feel limp and relaxed . . .

(REPEAT)

'Think about the muscles in your shoulders . . . Tense them by drawing up your shoulders towards your ears and pull them in towards your spine . . . Feel the tension across your shoulders and in your neck . . . Tense the muscles in your neck further by tipping your head back slightly . . . Hold the tension . . . Now relax . . . Let your head drop forward . . . Let your shoulders drop . . . Let them drop even further . . . Feel the tension easing away from your neck and shoulders . . . Feel your muscles relaxing more and more deeply . . . Your neck is limp and your shoulders feel heavy . . .

(REPEAT)

'Think about your face muscles . . . Focus on the muscles running across your forehead . . . Tense them by frowning as hard as you can . . . Hold that tension and focus on your jaw muscles . . . Tense the muscles by biting hard . . . Feel your jaw muscles tighten . . . Feel the tension in your face . . . Across your forehead . . . Behind your eyes . . . In your jaw . . . Now let go . . . Relax your forehead and drop your jaw . . . Feel the strain easing . . . Feel the tension draining away from your face . . . Your forehead feels smooth and relaxed . . . Your jaw is heavy and loose . . . Imagine the tension leaving your face . . . Leaving your neck . . . Draining away from your shoulders . . . Your head, neck, and shoulders feel heavy and relaxed.

(REPEAT)

'Think of your whole body now . . . Your entire body feels heavy and relaxed . . . Let go of any tension . . . Imagine the tension flowing out of your body . . . Listen to the sound of your calm, even breathing . . . Your arms, legs and head feel pleasantly heavy . . . Too heavy to move . . . You may feel as though you are floating . . . Let it happen . . . It is part of being relaxed . . .

'When images drift into your mind, don't fight them . . . Just acknowledge them and let them pass . . . You are a bystander: interested but not involved . . . Enjoy the feelings of relaxation for a few more moments . . . If you like, picture something that gives you pleasure and a sense of calm . . .

'In a moment, I will count backwards from four to one . . . When I reach one, open your eyes and lie still for a little while before you begin to move around again . . . You will feel pleasantly relaxed and refreshed . . .

'Four: beginning to feel more alert . . . Three: getting ready to start moving again . . . Two: aware of your surroundings . . . One: eyes open, feeling relaxed and alert.'

Exercise 2: Shortened progressive muscular relaxation

When you can use the first exercise successfully, you can shorten the routine by missing out the tensing stage.

Instructions

'You are relaxing . . . Breathe out slowly . . . Now, breathe in smoothly and deeply . . . Now, breathe out slowly again, imagining yourself becoming heavier and heavier, sinking into the floor (or your chair) . . . Keep breathing rhythmically, and feel a sense of relief and of letting go . . . Try saying "relax" to yourself as you breathe out . . . Breathe like this for a few moments more . . .

(READ ONCE)

'Now, begin to relax the muscles of your body . . . Think of your feet . . . Let your feet go limp and floppy . . . Feel the tension draining away from your feet . . . Let your feet roll outwards and grow heavier and heavier . . . Imagine that they are so heavy that they are sinking into the floor . . . More and more relaxed . . . growing heavier and more relaxed . . .

(REPEAT)

'Now, think about your calves . . . Let your feet touch the floor and let your legs go floppy and heavy . . . Feel the tension leaving your legs, draining away from your calves . . . Leaving your calves feeling heavy . . . Draining away from your feet ... Leaving them feeling heavy and limp ... Imagine that your legs and feet are so heavy that they are sinking into the floor ... They feel limp and relaxed ... Growing more and more heavy and relaxed ...

(REPEAT)

'Think about your thigh muscles ... Feel the tension draining away from your legs ... They feel limp and heavy ... Your thighs feel heavy ... Your calves feel heavy ... Your feet feel heavy ... Imagine the tension draining away ... Leaving your legs ... Leaving them feeling limp and relaxed ... Leaving them feeling so heavy that they are sinking into the floor (or your chair) ... Let the feelings of relaxation spread up from your feet ... Up through your legs ... Relaxing your hips and lower back ...

(REPEAT)

'Now relax the muscles of your hips, and lower back ... If you feel tension, let it go ... Let your muscles relax ... Feel your spine supported ... Feel the muscles relax ... Deeper and deeper ... More and more relaxed ... Growing heavier and heavier ... Your hips are relaxed ... Your legs are relaxed ... Your feet are heavy ... Tension is draining away from your body

(REPEAT)

'Relax your stomach and chest muscles ... As you breathe out, let go of your tension ... Feel your stomach muscles relax ... Feel the tightness leave your chest ... As you breathe evenly and calmly, your chest and stomach should gently rise and fall ... Allow your breathing to become rhythmic and relaxed ...

(REPEAT)

'Now think about your hands and arms ... Gently drop your arms by your side and imagine the tension draining away from your arms ... Leaving your upper arms ... Leaving your forearms ... Draining away from your hands ... Your arms feel heavy and floppy ... Your arms feel limp and relaxed ...

(REPEAT)

'Think about the muscles in your shoulders ... Now relax ... Let your head drop forward ... Let your shoulders drop ... Let them drop even further ... Feel the tension easing away from your neck and shoulders ... Feel your muscles relaxing more and more deeply ... Your neck is limp and your shoulders feel heavy ...

(REPEAT)

'Think about your face muscles ... Focus on the muscles running across your forehead ... Relax your forehead and drop your jaw ... Feel the strain easing ... Feel the tension draining away from your face ... Your forehead feels smooth and relaxed ... Your jaw is heavy and loose ... Imagine the tension leaving your face ... Leaving your neck ... Draining away from your shoulders ... Your head, neck, and shoulders feel heavy and relaxed ...

(REPEAT)

'Think of your whole body now . . . Your entire body feels heavy and relaxed . . . Let go of any tension . . . Imagine the tension flowing out of your body . . . Listen to the sound of your calm, even breathing . . . Your arms, legs and head feel pleasantly heavy . . . Too heavy to move . . . You may feel as though you are floating . . . Let it happen . . . It is part of being relaxed . . .

'When images drift into your mind, don't fight them . . . Just acknowledge them and let them pass . . . You are a bystander: interested but not involved . . . Enjoy the feelings of relaxation for a few more moments . . . If you like, picture something which gives you pleasure and a sense of calm . . .

'In a moment, I will count backwards from four to one . . . When I reach one, open your eyes and lie still for a little while before you begin to move around again . . . You will feel pleasantly relaxed and refreshed . . .

'Four: beginning to feel more alert . . . Three: getting ready to start moving again . . . Two: aware of your surroundings . . . One: eyes open, feeling relaxed and alert.'

Exercise 3: Simple relaxation routine

You can use an even shorter exercise, which you can practise at almost any time you need to. For the shorter routine, you have to imagine a mental image or mental device to use during the relaxation exercise. This can be a pleasant, calming scene, such as a deserted beach; a particularly relaxing picture or object; or sound or word which you find soothing, like the sound of the sea or the word 'serene'. The important thing is that you should find a mental device that is calming for you.

From time to time, distracting thoughts will come into your mind – this is quite usual. Don't dwell on them, simply return to thinking about your soothing image or sound. Once you have started the exercise, carry on for 10 to 20 minutes and, when you have finished, sit quietly with your eyes closed for a few moments. When you open your eyes, don't begin moving around too quickly.

To start the exercise, sit in a comfortable position. First, focus on your breathing. Take a slow, deep breath in . . . Feel the muscle beneath your rib cage move . . . Now let it out – slowly . . . Aim for a smooth pattern of breathing.

Instructions

'Close your eyes, and, while you continue to breathe slowly, imagine your body becoming more heavy . . . Scan your body for tension . . . Start at your feet and move up through your body to your shoulders and head . . . If you find any tension, try to relax that part of your body . . . Now, while your body is feeling as heavy and comfortable as possible, become aware of your breathing again . . . Breathe in through your nose, and fill your lungs fully . . . Now, breathe out again and bring to mind your tranquil image or sound . . . Breathe easily and naturally as you do this . . . Again, breathe in through your nose, filling your lungs . . . and out, thinking of your soothing mental device . . . When you are ready to breathe in again, repeat the cycle ... Keep repeating this cycle until you feel relaxed and calm and refreshed.

'When you have finished this exercise, sit quietly for a few moments, and enjoy the feeling of relaxation.'

An A–Z of worries, fears and anxieties

Earlier in this book, I said that fears and phobias were numerous and varied. The A–Z lists just some of the most common fears and might help you to identify your phobia more easily. Once you have labelled your fear, it is important that you remember that this is only a first step in the management of your problem. You must then understand exactly what it is that you fear so that you can devise your personal management plan. For example 'agoraphobia' is a useful label to describe the common fear of leaving a safe base. However, the origin of the fear can be varied. One person might experience agoraphobia because she has panic attacks in public places and her phobia will be best managed through learning how to control panic and through graded exposure to public places. Another person's agoraphobia might occur because he fears that something terrible will happen to his home in his absence and his fear is best helped by learning distraction and thought challenging. Yet someone else's agoraphobia might arise because she is frightened of being embarrassed in public and so lacks social confidence that she has become house-bound. In this case, assertivness training would be most helpful.

Whatever your fear, it can be understood and it can be overcome.

Agoraphobia

Strictly speaking, agoraphobia means 'fear of the market place' – a fear of open spaces. In fact, sufferers most often experience it as a fear of venturing from a place that feels safe, and the best way of overcoming agoraphobia is to leave the safe base as often as possible.

Blood phobia (haematophobia)

Blood phobia is different from other fears because it does not result in the usual increase in blood pressure which is associated with phobias. For all of us, the sight of blood causes a *drop* in blood pressure, which is why a person can feel light-headed and faint. The treatment of blood phobia is essentially the same as for other fears, except applied *tension* is used rather than applied relaxation. Instead of relaxing in response to unpleasant bodily symptoms, a person learns to tense muscles and raise blood pressure.

Claustrophobia

This is a fear of being in an enclosed space (a lift, a small room, the middle of a row in the theatre) and is often associated with a fear of panic attack and anticipation of not being able to escape. The management of claustrophobia involves learning to cope with panic, combined with exposure to difficult situations.

Darkness phobia (nyctophobia)

This is common in children who have catastrophic fears of things happening in the night. The kindest way to help them is to explain that they are quite safe and to build up their confidence by leaving fewer and fewer lights on for them. This fear also affects some adults – often those who suffer from nightmares or traumatic memories. Although the gradual exposure to darkness can be helpful to adults, the management of nightmares and traumatic memories is likely to need specialist help.

Fear of flying (aerophobia)

There can be many reasons for a fear of flying – it can be a form of claustrophobia, a catastrophic fear of crashing or hijack, a fear of heights. It is important that the sufferer discovers the particular basis of the fear so that it can be managed appropriately.

Gynophobia

This is a fear of women; its counterpart is androphobia, a fear of men. Such fears are often an expression of social phobia but can sometimes be associated with interpersonal trauma in the past. When this is the case, specialist counselling or therapy can be helpful.

Height phobia (acrophobia)

We are all born with a fear of heights which we usually outgrow. Sometimes, we simply do not 'unlearn' this fear and it persists into adulthood. These innate fears can some-times be difficult to describe because they are so deeply rooted, yet they respond very well to graded exposure.

Insect phobia (entomophobia)

We are also born with a fear of crawling creatures, including insects, spiders and wasps. This fear is often experienced as an unpleasant 'creepy' sensation under the skin.

Lyssophobia

A fear of insanity is not uncommon among sufferers of severe worries, fears and anxiety. The mood changes and difficulty in thinking clearly can be misinterpreted as losing one's mental faculties. Of course, this perception will fuel the worry and set up a maintaining cycle of distress.

Mirror phobia (elsoptrophobia)

A person who avoids seeing her/himself in the mirror usually dislikes that image. This might be because of a real or an imagined disfigurement or ugliness. Such avoidance is almost invariably linked with low self-esteem and the sufferer might need expert help in overcoming his or her negative self-image.

Novelty phobia (neophobia)

Some are made anxious by new things or people. It is impor-tant to identify the meaning of the threat: perhaps the sufferer is socially phobic and new people are particularly frightening; perhaps the sufferer fears failure and predicts not coping in a new situation. Once clarified, the neophobic person can begin to face the fear.

Ornithophobia

This is a fear of birds. Most commonly it is a dislike of the flapping movement of the animal and is often accompanied by vivid images of a bird being caught up in one's hair. In this respect, it is similar to bat phobias. Again, exposure to the feared object is the best form of treatment.

Pain phobia (algophobia)

Because stress is such a physical experience, this fear can actually bring on or worsen pain. The best remedy is to learn to relax and build up confidence that pain can be managed and can be bearable.

Reptile phobia (batrachophobia)

This is another of the fears that we seem to be born with and which some do not 'unlearn'. The most common of the batrachophobias is a fear of snakes, which is highly appropriate in some circumstances. As with all problem anxieties, when the fear is excessive or occurs out of context, the solution is anxiety management training.

School phobia (scholionophobia)

This is found in children and is almost always associated with unhappiness. Sometimes the child is the victim of bullying, sometimes s/he cannot keep up with the school work, sometimes the child has agoraphobia or social phobia. It is important that the parent or teachers help the child to feel safe enough to explain the fears.

Touch phobia (haptophobia)

A fear of touch might be associated with a fear of contamination, in which case exposure with thought challenging is the best intervention. Sometimes its roots are more sinister and the fear is associated with an abusive past. When this is the case, specialist counselling or therapy can be most helpful.

Vomit phobia (emetophobia)

This might reflect a fear of choking, a fear of being embarrassed in public or a fear of illness. Sufferers will avoid seeing others who might be sick (for example, avoiding hospitals and bars) because of the natural tendency of a witness to vomit feeling nauseous themselves. Again, management of emetophobia involves unpacking the fear and overcoming avoidance.

Weather phobias

The commonest weather-related fears are of lightning (astradophobia), of thunder (brontophobia) and of wind (anemophobia). The marked anxiety which is provoked by changes in the weather is usually associated with catastrophic predictions such as being struck by lightning, a roof being blown away or flooding. The sufferer needs to identify the meaning of the anxiety and begin to question its validity.

Xenophobia

This fear of foreigners or foreign countries might be a form of social phobia, a fear of novelty or simply a prejudice.

Useful books and addresses

Useful books

General

Adams, Ramona S. Herbert A. Otto and Deane S. Cowly, *Letting Go: Uncomplicating your life*, New York, Macmillan, 1980.

Bernhard, Yetta, *How to Be Somebody: Open the door to personal growth*, Millbrae, California, Celestial Arts, 1975.

Carson, Richard David, *Taming Your Gremlin: A guide to enjoying yourself*, Dallas, The Family Resource, 1983.

D. Burns, *The Feeling Good Handbook*, London, Plume, 1990.

G. Butler and A. Hope, *Manage Your Mind*, Oxford, Oxford University Press, 1995.

E. A. Charlesworth and R. G. Nathan, *Stress Management*, London, Corgi Books, 1987.

Donald W. Goodwin, *Anxiety*, New York & Oxford, Oxford University Press, 1986.

D. Greenberger and C. Padesky, *Mind over Mood*, London, Guilford Books, 1995

John H. Griest *et al.*, *Anxiety and Its Treatment*, New York, Warner Books, 1988.

Matthew McKay and Patrick Fanning, *Self-Esteem*, Oakland,

California, New Harbinger Publications, 1987.

J. W. Mills, *Coping with Stress*, Chichester, W. Sussex, Wiley 1982.

Hans Selye, *Stress without Distress*, Philadelphia, J. P. Lippincott, 1974.

Assertiveness

Robert E. Alberti and Michael L. Emmons, *Your Perfect Right: A guide to assertive living*, San Luis Obispo, California, Impact Publishers, 1982.

A. Dickson, *A Woman in Your Own Right*, London, Quartet Books, 1982.

W. Dyer, *Pulling Your Own Strings*, New York, Avon Books, 1979.

G. Lindenfield, *Assert Yourself*, London, Thorsons, 1986.

Mathew McKay, Martha Davis and Patrick Fanning, *Messages – The Communication Skills Book*, Oakland, California, New Harbinger Publications, 1985.

M. Smith, *When I Say No I feel Guilty*, New York, Bantam Books, 1976.

Time management

J. M. Atkinson, *Coping with Stress at Work*, London, Thorsons, 1988.

H. Reynolds and M. E. Tramel, *Executive Time Management*, Aldershot, Hants, Gower, 1979.

Useful addresses

United Kingdom

Institute for Neuro-Physiological Psychology
Warwick House
1 Stanley Street
CHESTER CH1 2LR
Tel: 01224 311414

MIND, The National Association for Mental Health
Granta House
15–19 Broadway
Stratford
LONDON E15 4BQ
Tel: 020 8519 2122 (can also give you details of local tran-
quillizer withdrawal support groups)

No Panic
93 Brands Farm Way
Randlay
TELFORD TF3 2JQ
Helpline: UK Free Phone: 0808 8080545
Non-UK: 0044 1952 590545

The Phobics Society (a self-help network for those with
phobias)
4 Cheltenham Road
Chorlton-cum-Hardy
MANCHESTER M21 1QN
Tel: 0161 8811937

Relaxation for Living Institute (courses and information to combat stress)
1 Great Chapel Street
LONDON W1F 8FA
Tel: 020 8671 1724

Stresswatch (workshops and information to deal with phobias and anxieties)
PO Box 4
LONDON W1A 4AR
(No telephone number available)
www.stresswatch.co.uk

Triumph Over Phobia
TOP U.K.
PO Box 3760
BATH BA2 3WY
Tel: 0845 6009601
email: info@topuk.org

Open Door Association (information for those with agoraphobia and anxieties)
447 Pensby Road
Heswall
Wirral
MERSEYSIDE LR1 9PQ
(No telephone number available)

Release (advice and information on drug use and abuse)
388 Old Street
LONDON EC1V 9LT
Tel: 020 7749 4044
Helpline: 0845 4500 215
email: ask@release.org.uk

USA

American Mental Health Foundation
2 East 86th Street
New York
NY 1008
Tel: 212 737 9027
elomke@americanhealthfoundation.org

Association for the Advancement of Behavior Therapy
305 7th Avenue
New York
NY 10001
Tel: 212 647 1890

Behavior Therapy of New York
51 East 42nd Street, Suite 1400
New York, NY 10017
Tel: (646) 522-7795
Email: inquire@behaviortherapy.com

Behavior Therapy Institute
San Francisco
Tel: 415 989 2140

Behavioral Psychotherapy Center
23 Old Mamaroneck Road
White Plains
NY 10605
Tel: 914 761 4080

Institute for Behavior Therapy
104 East 40th Street
New York
NY 10016
Tel: 212 692 9288
Toll free: 888 484 2111

Institutes for Neuro-Physiological Psychology:
Dr Larry J. Beuret, MD
4811 Emerson, Suite 209
Palatine
IL 60067
Tel: 847 303 1800
and

Mrs Victoria Hutton
6535 North Shore Way
Newmarket
Maryland 21774
Tel: 301 607 6752

White Plains Hospital Center
Anxiety and Phobia Clinic
Davis Ave., at Post Road
White Plains
NY 10601
Clinic tel.: 914 6810600
(Mon, Wed, Fri only, 9.00 a.m.-4.oo p.m.

Australia and New Zealand

Triumph Over Phobia
TOP NSW
PO BOX 213
Rockdale
New South Wales 2216

Institutes for Neuro-Physiological Research:
Dr Mary Lou Sheil
80 Alexandra Street
Hunters Hill 2110
Sydney, Australia
Tel: 298 796 596

Index

Note: page numbers in italic refer to illustrations or examples. The letter 't' after a page number refers to tables. Where more than one page number is listed against a heading, page numbers in bold indicate significant treatment of a subject

Extra diary sheets

Diary 1 Logging Stress reactions

Monitor your stress levels each day, noting when you feel particularly worried, frightened or anxious. Use the diary as near to the time of distress as possible as it is easy to forget the details later. Record the occasion and rate the severity of your feelings (1–10). Where you can, note what triggered the stress – thoughts, images, feelings, events, for example. Also, record how you tried to cope, and afterwards, rerate your distress levels.

Rate your distress on the following scale:

| 1 | 2 | 3 | 4 | 5 | 6 | 7 | 8 | 9 | 10 |

No distress, calm   Moderate distress   Absolute panic

Date, time	What was the occasion?	Rating	What brought it on?	How did you try to cope?	Rerating

Diary 1 Logging Stress reactions

Monitor your stress levels each day, noting when you feel particularly worried, frightened or anxious. Use the diary as near to the time of distress as possible as it is easy to forget the details later. Record the occasion and rate the severity of your feelings (1–10). Where you can, note what triggered the stress – thoughts, images, feelings, events, for example. Also, record how you tried to cope, and afterwards, rerate your distress levels.

Rate your distress on the following scale:

| 1 | 2 | 3 | 4 | 5 | 6 | 7 | 8 | 9 | 10 |

No distress, calm   Moderate distress   Absolute panic

Date, time	What was the occasion?	Rating	What brought it on?	How did you try to cope?	Rerating

Diary 1 Logging Stress reactions

Monitor your stress levels each day, noting when you feel particularly worried, frightened or anxious. Use the diary as near to the time of distress as possible as it is easy to forget the details later. Record the occasion and rate the severity of your feelings (1–10). Where you can, note what triggered the stress – thoughts, images, feelings, events, for example. Also, record how you tried to cope, and afterwards, rerate your distress levels.

Rate your distress on the following scale:

| 1 | 2 | 3 | 4 | 5 | 6 | 7 | 8 | 9 | 10 |

No distress, calm   Moderate distress   Absolute panic

Date, time	What was the occasion?	Rating	What brought it on?	How did you try to cope?	Rerating

Diary 1 Logging Stress reactions

Monitor your stress levels each day, noting when you feel particularly worried, frightened or anxious. Use the diary as near to the time of distress as possible as it is easy to forget the details later. Record the occasion and rate the severity of your feelings (1–10). Where you can, note what triggered the stress – thoughts, images, feelings, events, for example. Also, record how you tried to cope, and afterwards, rerate your distress levels.

Rate your distress on the following scale:

1	2	3	4	5	6	7	8	9	10

No distress, calm   Moderate distress   Absolute panic

Date, time	What was the occasion?	Rating	What brought it on?	How did you try to cope?	Rerating

Diary 1 Logging Stress reactions

Monitor your stress levels each day, noting when you feel particularly worried, frightened or anxious. Use the diary as near to the time of distress as possible as it is easy to forget the details later. Record the occasion and rate the severity of your feelings (1–10). Where you can, note what triggered the stress – thoughts, images, feelings, events, for example. Also, record how you tried to cope, and afterwards, rerate your distress levels.

Rate your distress on the following scale:

1	2	3	4	5	6	7	8	9	10

No distress, calm   Moderate distress   Absolute panic

Date, time	What was the occasion?	Rating	What brought it on?	How did you try to cope?	Rerating

Diary 2 Logging relaxation techniques

Record your level of relaxation before and after each exercise (1–10). Note any relevant information, such as the sort of day you are having, where you are, things on your mind. Use your record to discover where and when you are best able to relax and to monitor your progress.

Rate your distress on the following scale:

1	2	3	4	5	6	7	8	9	10

Not relaxed, tense   Moderate relaxation   Very relaxed, no tension

Date, time	Rating before	Which exercise did you use?	Rating afterwards	Notes

Diary 2 Logging relaxation techniques

Record your level of relaxation before and after each exercise (1–10). Note any relevant information, such as the sort of day you are having, where you are, things on your mind. Use your record to discover where and when you are best able to relax and to monitor your progress.

Rate your distress on the following scale:

1	2	3	4	5	6	7	8	9	10

Not relaxed, tense   Moderate relaxation   Very relaxed, no tension

Date, time	Rating before	Which exercise did you use?	Rating afterwards	Notes

Diary 2 Logging relaxation techniques

Record your level of relaxation before and after each exercise (1–10). Note any relevant information, such as the sort of day you are having, where you are, things on your mind. Use your record to discover where and when you are best able to relax and to monitor your progress.

Rate your distress on the following scale:

1	2	3	4	5	6	7	8	9	10

Not relaxed, tense   Moderate relaxation   Very relaxed, no tension

Date, time	Rating before	Which exercise did you use?	Rating afterwards	Notes

Diary 2 Logging relaxation techniques

Record your level of relaxation before and after each exercise (1–10). Note any relevant information, such as the sort of day you are having, where you are, things on your mind. Use your record to discover where and when you are best able to relax and to monitor your progress.

Rate your distress on the following scale:

1	2	3	4	5	6	7	8	9	10

Not relaxed, tense   Moderate relaxation   Very relaxed, no tension

Date, time	Rating before	Which exercise did you use?	Rating afterwards	Notes

Diary 2 Logging relaxation techniques

Record your level of relaxation before and after each exercise (1–10). Note any relevant information, such as the sort of day you are having, where you are, things on your mind. Use your record to discover where and when you are best able to relax and to monitor your progress.

Rate your distress on the following scale:

1	2	3	4	5	6	7	8	9	10
Not relaxed, tense			Moderate relaxation						Very relaxed, no tension

Date, time	Rating before	Which exercise did you use?	Rating afterwards	Notes

Diary 3 Thought diary

Monitor your stress levels each day, noting when you feel particularly worried, frightened or anxious. Use the diary as near to the time of distress as possible as it is easy to forget the details later. Rate the severity of your feelings (1–10) and note what thoughts or images triggered the distress. Then look for thinking biases and try to challenge your stress-provoking thoughts. Afterwards, rerate your distress level.

Rate your distress on the following scale:

1	2	3	4	5	6	7	8	9	10

No distress, calm   Moderate distress   Absolute panic

Date, time	What was going through your mind?	Rating	Thinking biases	How can you challenge this?	Rerating

Diary 3 Thought diary

Monitor your stress levels each day, noting when you feel particularly worried, frightened or anxious. Use the diary as near to the time of distress as possible as it is easy to forget the details later. Rate the severity of your feelings (1–10), and note what thoughts or images triggered the distress. Then look for thinking biases and try to challenge your stress-provoking thoughts. Afterwards, rerate your distress level.

Rate your distress on the following scale:

1	2	3	4	5	6	7	8	9	10

No distress, calm   Moderate distress   Absolute panic

Date, time	What was going through your mind?	Rating	Thinking biases	How can you challenge this?	Rerating

Diary 3 Thought diary

Monitor your stress levels each day, noting when you feel particularly worried, frightened or anxious. Use the diary as near to the time of distress as possible as it is easy to forget the details later. Rate the severity of your feelings (1–10), and note what thoughts or images triggered the distress. Then look for thinking biases and try to challenge your stress-provoking thoughts. Afterwards, rerate your distress level.

Rate your distress on the following scale:

1	2	3	4	5	6	7	8	9	10

No distress, calm   Moderate distress   Absolute panic

Date, time	What was going through your mind?	Rating	Thinking biases	How can you challenge this?	Rerating

Diary 3 Thought diary

Monitor your stress levels each day, noting when you feel particularly worried, frightened or anxious. Use the diary as near to the time of distress as possible as it is easy to forget the details later. Rate the severity of your feelings (1–10) and note what thoughts or images triggered the distress. Then look for thinking biases and try to challenge your stress-provoking thoughts. Afterwards, rerate your distress level.

Rate your distress on the following scale:

1	2	3	4	5	6	7	8	9	10

No distress, calm   Moderate distress   Absolute panic

Date, time	What was going through your mind?	Rating	Thinking biases	How can you challenge this?	Rerating

Diary 3 Thought diary

Monitor your stress levels each day, noting when you feel particularly worried, frightened or anxious. Use the diary as near to the time of distress as possible as it is easy to forget the details later. Rate the severity of your feelings (1–10), and note what thoughts or images triggered the distress. Then look for thinking biases and try to challenge your stress-provoking thoughts. Afterwards, rerate your distress level.

Rate your distress on the following scale:

1	2	3	4	5	6	7	8	9	10
No distress, calm				Moderate distress					Absolute panic

Date, time	What was going through your mind?	Rating	Thinking biases	How can you challenge this?	Rerating

Diary 4	Achievement record		
Date	Task	Anxiety rating (1–10)	Other relevant information

Diary 4	Achievement record		
Date	Task	Anxiety rating (1–10)	Other relevant information

Diary 4	Achievement record		
Date	Task	Anxiety rating (1–10)	Other relevant information

Diary 5 Sleep diary

Record the date and note any events which might affect your ability to sleep. For example, the food you ate before retiring, your stress levels, your activity just before going to bed, and so on. If you wake, note what you did to get back to sleep and whether or not this was helpful. Next day, note how many hours sleep you had and rate your level of alertness (Rating 1) and how well you performed during the day (Rating 2), using the following scales.

1. Alertness:

1	2	3	4	5	6	7	8	9	10

Not at all alert   Reasonably alert   Very alert

2. Performance:

1	2	3	4	5	6	7	8	9	10

Poor performance   Moderate performance   Performed well

Date	Notes	Waking episodes	Activity if not asleep: helpful Y/N	Hours sleep	Rating 1	Rating 2

Diary 5 Sleep diary

Record the date and note any events which might affect your ability to sleep. For example, the food you ate before retiring, your stress levels, your activity just before going to bed, and so on. If you wake, note what you did to get back to sleep and whether or not this was helpful. Next day, note how many hours sleep you had and rate your level of alertness (Rating 1) and how well you performed during the day (Rating 2), using the following scales.

1. Alertness:

| 1 | 2 | 3 | 4 | 5 | 6 | 7 | 8 | 9 | 10 |

Not at all alert   Reasonably alert   Very alert

2. Performance:

| 1 | 2 | 3 | 4 | 5 | 6 | 7 | 8 | 9 | 10 |

Poor performance   Moderate performance   Performed well

Date	Notes	Waking episodes	Activity if not asleep: helpful Y/N	Hours sleep	Rating 1	Rating 2

Diary 5 Sleep diary

Record the date and note any events which might affect your ability to sleep. For example, the food you ate before retiring, your stress levels, your activity just before going to bed, and so on. If you wake, note what you did to get back to sleep and whether or not this was helpful. Next day, note how many hours sleep you had and rate your level of alertness (Rating 1) and how well you performed during the day (Rating 2), using the following scales.

1. Alertness:

1	2	3	4	5	6	7	8	9	10

Not at all alert   Reasonably alert   Very alert

2. Performance:

1	2	3	4	5	6	7	8	9	10

Poor performance   Moderate performance   Performed well

Date	Notes	Waking episodes	Activity if not asleep: helpful Y/N	Hours sleep	Rating 1	Rating 2

Diary 5 Sleep diary

Record the date and note any events which might affect your ability to sleep. For example, the food you ate before retiring, your stress levels, your activity just before going to bed, and so on. If you wake, note what you did to get back to sleep and whether or not this was helpful. Next day, note how many hours sleep you had and rate your level of alertness (Rating 1) and how well you performed during the day (Rating 2), using the following scales.

1. Alertness:

1	2	3	4	5	6	7	8	9	10
Not at all alert				Reasonably alert					Very alert

2. Performance:

1	2	3	4	5	6	7	8	9	10
Poor performance				Moderate performance					Performed well

Date	Notes	Waking episodes	Activity if not asleep: helpful Y/N	Hours sleep	Rating 1	Rating 2

Diary 5 Sleep diary

Record the date and note any events which might affect your ability to sleep. For example, the food you ate before retiring, your stress levels, your activity just before going to bed, and so on. If you wake, note what you did to get back to sleep and whether or not this was helpful. Next day, note how many hours sleep you had and rate your level of alertness (Rating 1) and how well you performed during the day (Rating 2), using the following scales.

1. Alertness:

| 1 | 2 | 3 | 4 | 5 | 6 | 7 | 8 | 9 | 10 |

Not at all alert   Reasonably alert   Very alert

2. Performance:

| 1 | 2 | 3 | 4 | 5 | 6 | 7 | 8 | 9 | 10 |

Poor performance   Moderate performance   Performed well

Date	Notes	Waking episodes	Activity if not asleep: helpful Y/N	Hours sleep	Rating 1	Rating 2

More psychology titles from Constable & Robinson
Please visit www.overcoming.co.uk for more information

No.	Title	RRP	Offer price	Total
	An Introduction to Coping with Anxiety	£2.99	£2.00	
	An Introduction to Coping with Depression	£2.99	£2.00	
	An Introduction to Coping with Health Anxiety	£2.99	£2.00	
	An Introduction to Coping with Obsessive Compulsive Disorder	£2.99	£2.00	
	An Introduction to Coping with Panic	£2.99	£2.00	
	An Introduction to Coping with Phobias	£2.99	£2.00	
	Overcoming Anger and Irritability	£10.99	£8.99	
	Overcoming Anorexia Nervosa	£10.99	£8.99	
	Overcoming Anxiety	£10.99	£8.99	
	Overcoming Anxiety Self-Help Course (3 parts)	£21.00	£18.00	
	Overcoming Body Image Problems	£10.99	£8.99	
	Overcoming Bulimia Nervosa and Binge-Eating – new edition	£10.99	£8.99	
	Overcoming Bulimia Nervosa and Binge-Eating Self-Help Course (3 parts)	£21.00	£18.00	
	Overcoming Childhood Trauma	£10.99	£8.99	
	Overcoming Chronic Fatigue	£10.99	£8.99	
	Overcoming Chronic Pain	£10.99	£8.99	
	Overcoming Compulsive Gambling	£10.99	£8.99	
	Overcoming Depersonalizaton and Feelings of Unreality	£10.99	£8.99	
	Overcoming Depression – new edition	£10.99	£8.99	
	Overcoming Depression: Talks With Your Therapist (audio)	£10.99	£8.99	
	Overcoming Grief	£10.99	£8.99	
	Overcoming Health Anxiety	£10.99	£8.99	
	Overcoming Insomnia and Sleep Problems	£10.99	£8.99	
	Overcoming Low Self-Esteem	£10.99	£8.99	
	Overcoming Low Self-Esteem Self-Help Course (3 parts)	£21.00	£18.00	
	Overcoming Mood Swings	£10.99	£8.99	
	Overcoming Obsessive Compulsive Disorder	£10.99	£8.99	
	Overcoming Panic and Agoraphobia	£10.99	£8.99	
	Overcoming Panic and Agoraphobia Self-Help Course (3 parts)	£21.00	£18.00	
	Overcoming Paranoid and Suspicious Thoughts	£10.99	£8.99	

More psychology titles from Constable & Robinson (continued)

No.	Title	RRP	Offer price	Total
	Overcoming Problem Drinking	£10.99	£8.99	
	Overcoming Relationship Problems	£10.99	£8.99	
	Overcoming Sexual Problems	£10.99	£8.99	
	Overcoming Social Anxiety and Shyness	£10.99	£8.99	
	Overcoming Social Anxiety and Shyness Self-Help Course (3 parts)	£21.00	£18.00	
	Overcoming Stress	£10.99	£8.99	
	Overcoming Traumatic Stress	£10.99	£8.99	
	Overcoming Weight Problems	£10.99	£8.99	
	Overcoming Worry	£10.99	£8.99	
	Overcoming Your Child's Fears and Worries	£10.99	£8.99	
	Overcoming Your Child's Shyness and Social Anxiety	£10.99	£8.99	
	Overcoming Your Smoking Habit	£10.99	£8.99	
	The Compassionate Mind	£20.00	£15.00	
	The Happiness Trap	£9.99	£7.99	
	The Glass Half-Full	£8.99	£7.99	
	I Had a Black Dog	£6.99	£5.24	
	Living with a Black Dog	£7.99	£5.99	
	Manage Your Mood: How to use Behavioral Activation Techniques to Overcome Depression	£12.99	£9.99	
	P&P		FREE	FREE
	TOTAL			

Name (block letters): _____

Address: _____

_____ Postcode: _____

Email: _____ Tel No: _____

How to Pay:

1. By telephone: call the TBS order line on 01206 255 800 and quote KENNERLEY. Phone lines are open between Monday–Friday, 8.30am–5.30pm.

2. By post: send a cheque for the full amount payable to TBS Ltd, and send form to: Freepost RLUL-SJGC-SGKJ. Cash Sales/Direct Mail Dept, The Book Service, Colchester Road, Frating, Colchester, CO7 7DW

Is/are the book(s) intended for personal use ☐ or professional use ☐?
Please note this information will not be passed on to third parties.